the Shortage Survival Handbook

by George I. Karnaookh

BOOKS FOR BETTER LIVING • CHATSWORTH, CALIFORNIA

ISBN 0-88491-211-6

Library of Congress
Card Number: 74-80950

The Trident Principle is an empirically tested law that promises each and every one of us the choice of three, often overlapping, solutions to almost any shortage.

—George I. Karnaookh

CONTENTS

Preface 9

PART ONE:
    BEATING THE ENERGY CRISIS 15

Chapter
    1. Energy—and *Your* Home 19
    2. Fun, Food—and Energy 45
    3. On the Road 55

PART TWO:
    BEATING THE FOOD SHORTAGE .. 70

    4. When Supermarket Shelves Go Bare. 72
    5. Growing Your Own Vegetables ... 81
    6. Cooking Wisely 89
    7. Water, Water—Is It Everywhere? .. 96

PART THREE:
    GETTING AROUND THE
    HOUSING PINCH 105

    8. If You Want to Rent or Lease 107
    9. If You Want to Buy 116
    10. If You Want to Build 122
    11. Alternatives to the
        Standard Residence 130

PART FOUR:
THE COMET'S TAIL—
A MISCELLANY OF SHORTAGES ...139

12. Furnishings: Home and Personal ...141
13. The Question of
    Professional Services 148
14. End Your Money Woes 154

Conclusion 159

Appendixes 160

Index 166

Preface

Yes, we have no bananas, steaks, eggs, blue jeans,
candles, gas, tennis balls, freezers, wheat, leather,
air conditioners, fuel oil, pyjamas, floor covering,
sardines, chicken, paper, hot water bottles . . .
— The National Association of
Manufacturers poster

In the operating room there were whispered in-
troductions: "Dr. Remington, Dr. Mitty. Mr.
Pritchard-Mitford, Dr. Mitty." . . . A huge, com-
plicated machine, connected to the operating table,
with many tubes and wires, began at this moment
to go pocketa-pocketa-pocketa. "The new anes-
thetizer is giving way!" shouted an interne.
"There is no one in the East who knows how to
fix it!" "Quiet, man!" said Mitty, in a low, cool

9

voice. He sprang to the machine, which was now going pocketa-pocketa-queep-pocketa-queep. He began to finger a row of glistening dials. "Give me a fountain pen!" he snapped. Someone gave him a fountain pen. He pulled a faulty piston out of the machine and inserted the pen in its place. "That will hold for ten minutes," he said. "Get on with the operation."

—James Thurber, *The Secret Life of Walter Mitty*

What in the world, you might ask, does the National Association of Manufacturers have to do with the *Secret Life of Walter Mitty* and what does the *Secret Life of Walter Mitty* have to do with you? To draw a direct analogy from the National Association of Manufacturers, Walter Mitty, and you and me, and all of us "consumers": The frivolous National Association of Manufacturers poster is advising us that the *pocketa-pocketa-pocketa* rhythm of our lives is about to go not just *pocketa-pocketa-queep*— but *queep-queep-queep!* This situation is to Walter Mitty what *inefficiency* is to *ingenuity*. And Walter Mitty is to you what *ingenuity* is to *survival*—comfortable survival—in a world about to enter the Age of Shortages. We have just passed the threshold into that era, and felt the passing as "the energy crisis."

But the crisis is over, you might say. The fuel shortage has been solved. There are no more lines at the service stations.

The grocery shelves are beginning to show fewer and fewer gaps. Of course, the prices are still rising, but some items—meat, for example—you say, are becoming less expensive. We've even succeeded in approaching Zero Population Growth this year!

It *is* tempting to look at it that way, to bear down on the gas pedal again and hit 65, 70, 75, 80 miles per hour, to say, "Thank God, it's over," while continuing to pay constantly escalating prices for practically everything that is available.

Consider current, post-fuel crisis news items and ads such as: *"Economics of Scarcity May Be Replacing Era of Plenty in U.S."* (Los Angeles Times headline, April 21, 1974); *"Worldwide Shortage of Grain Seen:* A worldwide grain shortage next year could force Americans to choose between eating less meat or letting Asians and Africans starve, an international food specialist [Lester R. Brown of the Overseas Development Council] says" *(Los Angeles Herald-Examiner,* April 26, 1974); *"Oil Embargo Ended, Fuel Crisis Ended. Baloney.* The oil embargo is ended . . . for now. But the fuel crisis is as grave as ever" (American Electric Power System ad appearing in various news magazines).

Of course, we have had warnings of Armageddon: God knows when, there was the Apocalypse of St. John the Divine; in 1948 there was Fairfield Osborne's *Our Plundered Planet,* in 1954 Harrison Brown's *The Challenge of Man's Future,* in 1968 Dr. Paul R. Ehrlich's *The Population Bomb,* and in 1970 Gordon Rattray Taylor's *The Doomsday Book,* to mention but a few. Yet, these warnings have failed to provoke those in a position to *act* and through their action to forestall the arrival of the Thurberesque *queep* in our *pocketa* of plenty.

It is not the object of this book to point the finger of blame for the shortages at any conglomerate or monopoly. However, shortages (past, present, and future), considering the current advanced state of technology, are the end result of inefficient production; and in some cases, as we have learned during the fuel shortage, this inefficiency has proven to be extraordinarily profitable. This is a frightening realization—for the consumer. Hence, this book.

It is a "you-can-get-it-if-you-want-it" guide for anyone who has become discouraged by the sporadically barren shelves that greet the eye at our supermarkets. It is also a practical handbook for anyone, and everyone, who feels that the time has come for the consumer to strike back at those who manipulate him into a state of dependence on their product: Without much effort, we can find perfectly satisfactory substitutes.

In short, this is a manual on comfortable and enjoyable survival for anyone who has been made uncomfortable—or, in the the terminology of common journalese, "edgy"—by the initially frightening scarcity of everything from meat and potatoes to toilet paper, from grocery bags to housing, from gas to money, from time to temper, from the one-quart size of Clorox bleach to credibility. It is a simple Baedeker for anyone who wishes to find his or her way *easily* through the bumpercrop maze of shortages that we are led to believe is the harvest of our times.

Shortages are seldom anything more than artificial, manmade obstacles in the game of life. And the game of life, if one takes the obstacles in stride, *can* be— as this book will show—and *should* be a fun game with a capital F. All one needs to enjoy playing, and to win, that game is knowledge of how to get under, over, around, or through those obstacles without missing the rhythm or getting the blues.

"Nothing lies beyond human ingenuity" is the primary premise of this book. Lest this frighten you into thinking that a university extension course or an Einsteinian I.Q. is essential to outfox the obstacle-setters, it should be immediately pointed out that one need not be a genius to be ingenious. Furthermore, the germs of ingenuity are already liberally scattered throughout the pages of this book. They've been gathered from innumerable relevant published sources, from whispered hints overheard, and from the cultivation of ideas that sprang up during the researching and writing of this book.

Regardless of what you need, regardless of how "difficult" or "impossible" *they* say getting it is, regardless of what your previous personal experience has been in trying to get it, this book will show you not just when and where to go and how to get whatever it is that you want but also offer you several alternatives and save you either time or money, or both, in the process. If the item or commodity you want becomes not just *scarce* but actually *unavailable*, this book will either direct you to an item or commodity that will do as well as, or better than, the one you are unable to find, or it will show you how —through that human ingenuity of yours—to make or grow it yourself.

We are creatures of habit, and, whether we realize it or not, some of our habits are wasteful in more ways than one. Some thirteen years ago, Vance Packard, you may remember, wrote a very embarrassing book about the supply side of our supply-and-demand society, calling both his book and our industry *The Wastemakers*. The industry did not heed his warnings; they continued on their merry, profit-making way, progressing through "planned obsolescence and planned chaos," with the end result being that the consumer is now facing shortages.

"Waste not," then, "want not," is the secondary premise of this book. No, it is *not* a hoarder's handbook; hoarding, by its very definition, connotes a wasting through nonuse. Building and maintaining a reserve supply (of provisions in a freezer, or of gas in a drum in the garage, for example) is *not* hoarding, it is prudence, and will be discussed in this book, as will be methods of how to make those provisions and that gas last considerably longer than your habits have been allowing them to last until now.

With the cost of living escalating as it is, one of the most critical shortages that we all face is the shortage of cash. And the final bonus that this book offers is an inevitable saving method: Ingenuity and thriftiness add up to money in *your* purse!

This book offers you much more than the injunction, "Go, be ingenious and thrifty and you will want not." "Use your head and make a tight fist and you'll be happy," is so abstract that both Muhammad Ali and Ebenezer Scrooge could use it in teaching each other his respective trade.

The Trident Principle, however, *is not abstract.*

It is *real!*

It is your all-purpose anti-shortage tool.

If you are curious as to what it is, turn to Chapter One; if you want to know how it's used, keep reading.

PART ONE

BEATING THE ENERGY CRISIS

The nation's requirements for energy will about double between now and 1985. In this period, we shall have to rely upon oil, gas, coal, and nuclear power for at least 95% of our needs. If present trends continue, our indigenous resources of these materials will not be developed fast enough to meet our growing requirements. . . . We shall become increasingly dependent upon foreign countries, primarily in the Middle East. . . .

> —An address by John G. McLean,
> chairman and chief executive officer of
> Continental Oil Company,
> —*Time* (December 11, 1972)

*At his White House news conference last week,
President Nixon . . . went on to warn the Arabs
that if they continued their threats, they might
find . . . that their buyers had decided to go to
friendlier sellers. "Oil without a market," said
Nixon, ". . . doesn't do a country much good. . . ."*
—Time (September 17, 1973)

*Like a great natural disaster, the oil drought
caused by the Arabs' cutback on production
spread ominously through the industrial nations
last week. . . . Even more worrisome is the growing probability of acute oil shortages caused by
the Arabs' total embargo of oil shipments to the
U.S. . . .*
—Time (November 12, 1973)

*Provided Congress approves President Nixon's
requests, U.S. aid to Arab nations could amount
to half a billion dollars . . . in the fiscal year
that begins this July. . . .*
—Time (May 6, 1974)

*Nothing has angered consumerists more than the
huge profit increases that oil companies have
enjoyed during the energy crisis . . .: Shell, up
52% over the 1973 first quarter; Mobil, 66%;
Gulf, 76%; Standard of Indiana, 81%; Standard of Californa, 92%; Texaco, 123%; Continental, 130%; and Occidental, a stunning 718%.*
—Time (May 6, 1974)

*Although we have not exhausted our reserves,
nor run out of either domestic or imported oil,
every consumer can testify that there is a shortage at the pump or at the heating-oil supply
truck. We are forced to conclude that the short-*

age faced by consumers at the beginning of 1974
was artifical and contrived.

A statement by the Scientists' Institute
for Public Information,
—*Environment* (March 1974)

Chapter 1

Energy—and *Your* Home

Undoubtedly, even though there is no mention of it made by the author of Genesis, Adam and Eve used the Trident Principle in the Year Zero, i.e., during the time following their infamous eviction from the Garden of Eden by their Landlord for messing around with one of his snakes. Alexander Serkirk, sailing master of the privateer *Cinque Ports Galley,* who, at his own request, was left on the desolate island of Juan Fernandez off the coast of Chile for four years and four months (1704-1709), and on whose real-life adventures Defoe based his classic *Robinson Crusoe,* likewise made full use of it. So did—and do—countless others, day in and day out, seldom recognizing either their inherent ingenuity or the essentially simple and common-sensical rigidity of the Principle.

What *is* the Trident Principle? Basically, it is an empirically tested law that promises each and every one of us the choice of three, often overlapping, solutions to almost any shortage—regardless of whether that shortage be real or contrived.

The first of these is *conservation*, and should be ideally coupled at all times with *production* and what might be called *"neodevelopment."* Thus, replacing a 100-watt light bulb with one of 75-watt power is *conservation*. Rigging up a water wheel so that it is spun or rotated by the running waters of a stream or river, and which in turn drives a generator, which we tap for electricity, is *production*. Figuring out a way of utilizing geothermal steam to activate turbines to run generators to produce electricity for lighting that bulb is *neodevelopment*.

The second solution is *substitution*. Removing, for example, one of two 100-watt bulbs and substituting a high-reflectivity mirror for it is substitution. Proper placement of the mirror *can* provide almost as much illumination as another light bulb.

The third solution is *backtracking*. It involves doing nothing other than what the word implies— taking a position on the stepping-stone immediately preceding the one on which the shortage in question had become acute. Specifically in the case of electricity, for example, we can flick off the light switch and light a kerosene lamp, an oil lamp, or a candle.

Backtracking isn't as bad as it sounds. Difficult though it might be for most of us to accept, because of our technological conditioning, the fact remains that man had managed not just to survive extraordinarily well for thousands of years without the (often dubious) benefits of advanced technology, but to love, dream, create, think, and generally to enjoy life.

Doesn't that third solution—of backtracking—smack of atavism? No! Atavism is the pet bugaboo of industrialism. Neither dinner by candlelight nor life outdoors, in the wilds, is atavistic; uncontrolled armament, technological pollution, and wars, however, are. Atavism is not man's ability to do without modern, streamlined, labor-saving devices and contrivances; it is an emotional and mental apathy of man for mankind and of mankind for man. Men in sophisticatedly computerized, armored, anti-life vehicles thundering over land, speeding across and under water, or streaking through the air are not any less barbarian than the most primitive of the club-swinging cave-dwellers.

So let's take a firm grip on the Trident Principle and see how it can be utilized, to begin with, in beating the energy crisis in the home, whether home is a private house or an apartment. Since the greatest energy demand in any dwelling is for heating and cooling, let's start with that.

Heating and the Trident Principle

It makes absolutely no difference as far as the first element of the Trident Principle, *conservation*, goes whether your home is heated by a gas, oil, electric, steam, hot-water, or forced warm-air system, by *x*-number of fireplaces, or by a combination of any of these. The system, in other words, can vary, but the methods of conserving fuel, *by conserving heat*, are pretty much the same in all cases.

To make certain that there is no inadvertent wastage of fuel in the heating of your home, first check the size and rating of your furnace against what might be termed the "load" it is expected to carry, which is, in effect, the volume of the living space of your home that it is expected to maintain at a certain temperature.

21

This can be done either by a service representative of any reputable firm that specializes in heating and air-conditioning systems, *or* by yourself. If you have a knack for solving basically challenging problems made relatively simple in pamphlets or booklets that are available, in most cases for the asking, at most of the major chain stores that handle heating and air-conditioning systems (Montgomery Ward and Sears & Roebuck, for example, have excellent step-by-step guides to selecting a system that will be most efficient for your home), there is no reason in the world why you cannot do it yourself. It is only imperative that it be done, since proper rating (or capacity) of a furnace will eliminate the totally unnecessary wastage of fuel at the source. If you are a renter, it shouldn't be difficult to convince your landlord of the importance of such a check.

Assuming, then, that you have as close to a perfect balance between the power of the furnace and its load, you are ready to continue with your conservation campaign—which will be reflected in your next month's utilities bill—by checking out the following:

1. *Thermostat setting.* Select a setting for the temperature that is comfortable for you—it will probably be somewhere between 66 and 70° F.—*and forget about it!* In the words of A. M. Watkins, the nationally known consultant in the home-buying field, author of several "how to" books, and expert in his own right: "Don't fiddle with the thermostat." As a matter of fact, the only time it should be touched—and this, only to save energy and to cut down on the bill—is before you go away for a weekend, a vacation, or a business trip that will leave your home vacant for an extended period of time, and when you return. In the first case, turn the thermostat Off; in the second, turn it On.

Do *not*, upon returning from your trip, raise the

thermostat setting to 80 or 85 or 90° F., even though the chill that greets you at the door might very well tempt you to do so. This wasteful maneuver is not at all uncommon, but that is exactly what it is—a totally wasteful move. The thermostat setting has nothing to do with the heating rate of the furnace; it will take just as much time for the temperature inside your home to reach 70° with the thermostat set at 85° as it will if you leave it at 70°. But the wastage of fuel *will* occur because the furnace is going to burn fuel until the temperature in your living room reaches the thermostat setting—unless, which is not likely, you manage to "sense 70°" and turn the thermostat setting down to that figure.

2. *Insulation.* A. M. Watkins, in his extremely readable book, *The Homeowner's Survival Kit*—a book useful to renters as well as owners—offers a marvelous case for temperature (warm *or* cool) conservation, which *insulation* basically is: "You could heat your house with a candle or at practically no cost at all if it were built like a cold-storage room. That means walls, floor, and roof solidly packed with blocks of insulation so that an absolute minimum of heat can leak out.

"In such a house," he continues, "the windows would be built with at least three sheets of glass (triple storm-windows) with an inert air space between the glass layers. The doors would be sealed with refrigeratorlike gaskets. Outside air would be drawn in for ventilation, but it would be heated or cooled (also filtered) before being let in, according to the outdoor-air temperature."

Anyone who has seen the price of high-quality thermos, or vacuum, bottles will know that Watkins is making a marvelous point for insulation, an essential method of conserving heat at a reasonable price. The primary function of insulation is to arrest, or minimize, heat transfer; in simple terms, insulation keeps warm air from getting out of the house and cold air from getting in during the cold season, and vice versa during the warm.

Heating the great outdoors with your furnace is both futile and wasteful, but that is exactly what your heating system is doing if there is any air leakage between the interior of your dwelling and its exterior. A few simple steps can reduce such two-way air leakage.

When you make entrances and exits in your home or apartment, make them quickly. Do not, for example, open the door until *after* you've shaken the snow off your coat, until *after* you've wiped your rain-soaked and muddy shoes on the welcome mat, until *after* you've definitely decided that you are going to come in, or go out.

Check for air leakage at all windows and doors; these occur between window frames and masonry, between window sashes and window frames, and between the doors and their frames. Air leakages are easy to detect on cold or windy days and are not difficult to eliminate. Home improvement centers carry weather stripping—felt and rubberized strips of varying thickness—that is easy to install. If you follow the instructions on the package, you may have a problem *shutting* the window unless you select stripping of proper thickness. If you do run into this difficulty, the stripping, *after* it is installed, is relatively easy to trim until a snug fit is obtained. An X-acto knife or razor blade will do the job nicely— as long as you keep your fingers out of the razor's path.

Weather stripping also comes in lengths of thin spring bronze; pieces of this—cut to premeasured lengths—attached to the doors and window sashes so that they bear against their enclosing frames will keep that heat from getting out and the cold air from getting in. Spring bronze stripping is more attractive, however it is a bit more difficult to install; the instructions should be followed meticulously in this case. Unlike the felt and rubberized weather stripping, which *may* be installed *against,* or *over,* the crack between window sash and window frame, spring bronze has to be fastened *within* the breach.

If your winters are severe, your home probably is provided with storm windows. (It is curious that storm windows are seldom used in *hot* climates, since the insulation they provide works both against cold *and* hot temperatures.) If your storm windows are of the type where they fill the window opening and bear against the blind stops of the window frames, the chances are that you do not have to be concerned about air leakage. If, on the other hand, they are of the type that are clamped to the window sash and just cover the glass areas, check for air infiltration and be prepared to install weather stripping. The same holds true for double- or multiple-glazed window sashes—window sashes with two or more window-panes installed within them, thereby forming what might be called a glass-and-air "sandwich." Weather stripping will greatly enhance the effectiveness of their insulating properties.

Drapes over the windows, perferably extending out about six inches to a foot (or more) over the walls at the top and the sides, will further cut down on your heating system's efforts. Unless there is direct sunlight coming in through the windows, keep the drapes drawn shut. Of course, if your drapery is of a dark and heavy material, and drawing the drapes shut requires your switching on, and *not* needlessly, a light in every room, then leave the drapes open. If you need light in only one room, draw the drapes shut and turn *on* the light you need.

3. *Heating outlets.* If your home is heated by means of a forced warm-air system, there is more than likely a heating outlet in every room; if your system is electric, there may be several thermostats that can be regulated or switched on and off. But what about the previously mentioned instruction about not "fiddling" with the thermostat? Does this apply to heating outlets and a *number* of thermostats as well?

If the insulation in your home has been maximized by weather stripping, storm windows, and drapes (let's disregard heat loss through the walls, which in most cases is minimal), you can do better than close the heating outlets or switch off the individual thermostats in unoccupied rooms. You can—unless it's close to the freezing point (32° F.) outside—touch that untouchable thermostat (or thermostats) and turn the setting back about five degrees. It is very unlikely that you will notice any difference in temperature, but you will notice that you are burning considerably less fuel from that point on.

4. *The fireplace.* If you have one or more of these marvelous holes in the wall, consider yourself fortunate. Place some combustibles in its silent maw, strike a match, and you transform the hollow space into Original Heat. If it is not a gas-fed fireplace—as so many of the modern ones are—*it embodies all three elements of the Trident Principle.*

a. It *conserves* fuel, since it can be fed anything that will burn—and a great many daily discards, which we normally have gotten into the habit of trying to force into the overflowing trash cans, do and will burn: milk cartons, cereal boxes, soap cartons, frozen-food containers, old newspapers and magazines, mown grass (let it dry out for a few days), twigs, and branches, which are the inevitable remnants of a gardening and pruning job.

b. It *substitutes,* burning trash instead of conventional fuel. As a matter of fact, in *U.S. News & World Report* of March 11, 1974, we are advised that "trash heaps" may be our major new source of power: "The trash heaps of America hold enough fuel to ease materially the nation's energy crisis. A report just released by the Environmental Protection Agency claims that out of 130 million tons of refuse accumulated annually in the U.S., 75 percent could be burned to generate electricity or to heat and air-condition buildings. This combustible trash is the equivalent of 150 million barrels of oil." And 150 million barrels of oil, the article goes on to say, "could light all the homes and commercial buildings in the U.S. for a full year . . . equals one fifth of the crude oil to be supplied by the Alaskan pipeline in a 12-month period . . . is equivalent to 40 percent of the crude oil imported annually from the Mideast."

Keep in mind: Every 45-gallon trash can contains the equivalent of one gallon of oil! And you don't have to process that fuel to use it in your fireplace, other than separate the combustibles from the other trash.

c. It is the ultimate in *backtracking*. By feeding discards into the fireplace, we are taking ourselves all the way back to the days of our brilliant ancestor who discovered that fire gives off warmth.

And the utilizability of the fireplace does not stop with heating. It gives off light. Its flames can be used for preparing food (more on this subject later).

5. *Solar energy*. If you are an adventurous soul—particularly if you are planning on building a home, although conversion is also plausible—you might want to consider harnessing solar energy for heating your house. There is literature available on such projects from the National Science Foundation, and progressively more and more "how-to" articles have been cropping up in recent semi-technical periodicals.

Essentially, the system is simple: Solar collectors containing electricity-producing cells, also known as "black panels," absorb sun's heat and conduct it to a layer of circulating water directly beneath the panels. The water carries the heat to a "storage and heat exchanger" (a combination of metals that melts at a relatively low temperature or a simple water tank) and the heat can then be used on cold days to warm the air circulating around the building or, on hot days, to run an air-conditioning unit.

An alternative approach uses air instead of water to carry the heat to the heat storage unit. In both systems, the electricity produced by the solar collectors, in conjunction with a battery, can be used to run household appliances.

Utilization of solar energy is nothing new. One of the major attractions at the 1878 Paris Exposition was a steam engine that was powered by heat from the sun. Japanese, Australians, and Latin Americans have been using the sun for years to heat their bath water by simply storing it in rooftop tanks.

As of this writing, solar-heated homes have already been built in Denver, Lexington, Phoenix, and Washington; RCA Corporation has announced plans to construct a solar-heated addition atop its headquarters at Rockefeller Plaza in New York; a solar furnace in the French Pyrenees mirror-focuses the sun's rays effectively enough to produce temperatures as high as 3,500 degrees, high enough for simple industrial uses.

The other unconventional sources of energy are entirely out of the average person's reach, and appear to be slow in coming. Congress has appropriated $10 million for geothermal research and development; the government has recently leased federal lands in Colorado, Utah, and Wyoming for oil shale development; and experts estimate that nuclear energy will provide somewhere around 25% of our electrical production by 1985 and 50% by the year 2000.

Until such neodevelopments become commercially and ecologically feasible, our tangible sources of heat in the home will remain to be natural gas, electricity, and the fireplace. Our alternate choice will be the sun, and if we take a firm hold on its rays and a firmer grip on the Trident Principle, we should have no problem at all making it through the night of shortages.

Before turning to air conditioning (and most of the steps taken in conserving energy in *heating* a house or apartment apply in *cooling* as well), it should be pointed out that when you are *not* using the fireplace to provide heat, or light, close the fireplace damper, and, of course, follow the maintenance steps mentioned in your heater manufacturer's instruction booklet. A poorly maintained heating system is an energy-wasting system.

Air Conditioning and the Trident Principle

One of the most unique and admirable characteristics that the human body possesses is its ability not only to withstand extremes of heat and cold but to acclimatize itself to them. Nevertheless, in 1911, Dr. Willis H. Carrier, having come to the conclusion that "vapor pressure of an air-vapor mixture is always the pressure corresponding to that of saturated water vapor existing at its dew-point temperature," invented the air-conditioner. Now, it *is* a nice contraption to have—most air-conditioning units are not even unsightly when they are made invisible by concealment above the ceiling or behind walls—but do they *have* to be set to go on when the temperature in the home rises one or two degrees above the setting on our heating system's thermostat?

Let's consider the plethora of heating units, cooling

units, humidifying units, combination of this-and-that units—both those humming in the homes and those standing in stacks on sales floors just waiting for you to take them home so they can blow hot or cold air at you and humidify you and keep you surrounded by "normal temperature" and thermostats.

The impression one gets is that we have been thoroughly conditioned to feel "cold" at 69° and "hot" at 71°, or at whatever two temperatures proclaimed by the experts to be "normal" for us. One day I was driving with the air-conditioner on in the car. I was hot, perspiring, in fact. Then I saw a temperature sign on a building flash "68°." Automatically, I turned the air-conditioner off. *It was not hot enough yet to feel hot.*

In other words, in a great many instances we fall victim to the conditioning elements that surround us, and in no fewer instances to the air-conditioning elements. Consequently, applying the first phase of the Trident Principle, *conservation,* to the air-conditioner-in-the-home dilemma, the rule of thumb to follow ends with a question mark. Does it really get hot enough in your home during the hottest days of summer for you to feel uncomfortable! Unless there is a health problem, at which time a uniformly maintained temperature is required, forget about the myth of "normal" temperature. A human being an egg is not; lifetime incubation for us is not only unnecessary but can actually be harmful.

So the ultimate application of the *conservation* element of the Trident Principle to air conditioning overlaps the *backktracking element:* Unless you are uncomfortable, forget about your air-conditioner. Turn it off. See if you can condition yourself back to enjoying the warm days of summer. If you're hot, you're hot. Take a dip in a pool. Run through a sprinkler. Take a cold shower. Pour yourself a nice cold glass of

lemonade and sit in the shade. Think of an iceberg.
You may save as much as 2000 kilowatt-hours (the
average annual consumption of energy by an average
air-conditioner as determined by the Citizen's Advisory Committee in Environmental Quality in 1973),
which is the amount of energy a 100-watt light bulb
would consume if left burning for twenty-eight
months. As a matter of fact, an air-conditioner consumes more energy in a year's time than all the lights
you burn during that period.

Can't do it, you say. *It's too hot.* Well, switching
that air-conditioner off is the most efficient maneuver. But you can still conserve without taking
that step of flicking the switch. There is a whole
ladder of steps for throttling your air-conditioner's
appetite for energy.

Before taking those steps though, let's pause to
check and see if the air-conditioning system you have
(if you have one) is of the proper rating for what
you want it to do. If there is no cooling system in
your house or apartment and you are determined upon
buying one, the following simple bit of calculation
will tell you exactly what size unit you will need.

Just as the power of your car's engine is measured in units of "horsepower," the power (or "capacity") of an air-conditioner is measured in "British
thermal units" (B.T.U.). (A *British thermal unit* is
defined as *the quantity of heat required to raise the
temperature of one pound of water one degree Fahrenheit at or near 39.2° F*. In the case of *cooling*, it
can be defined as *the quantity of* refrigeration *required to* lower *the temperature of one pound of
water one degree Fahrenheit at or near 39.2° F.)*

Essentially, there are three factors that will determine the size (B.T.U. capacity) of air-conditioner for
your home—the size will be both the most economical
(in terms of cost and in terms of energy consump-

tion) and the most efficient. They are: 1) volume of living area to be cooled, 2) the average maximum temperature registered in your home without a cooling system, 3) the B.T.U. per cubic foot of air to be cooled factor, which depends on the second factor above and the values for which are listed in the table below.

Average Maximum Temperature Ranges
and Approximate Cooling Factors for Each

Temperature Range (°F.)	Cooling Factor
65 - 70	2.0
70 - 75	2.5
75 - 80	3.0
80 - 85	3.5
85 - 90	4.0
90 - 95	4.5
95 - 100	5.0
100 - 105	5.5

For example: You want a unit to cool your living and dining room areas. Your living room measures 13 by 21 feet; your dining room 11 by 14. The height of your ceilings is 8 feet, which is considered to be the average height of modern home ceilings. Multiply length by width by height: 21 x 13 x 8. You get the volume of your living room: 2184 cubic feet. The volume of your dining room is obtained the same way: 14 x 11 x 8 = 1232 cubic feet. Adding the volume of your living room to that of your dining room, you find that you want an air-conditioning unit (or units) that will cool a total volume of 3416 cubic feet.

Having checked the thermometer in your living room for the past five days, you know that the day's high has been between 85 and 90° F. The "cooling factor" for such temperatures, from the preceding table, is 4. Multiplying 3416 cubic feet (the total volume) by 4, gives you a figure of 13,664, which is your B.T.U. requirement. This means that a 14,000 B.T.U. air-conditioner unit (or two units that give you an equivalent total capacity) is what you need.

It is true that *two* units—a 9,000 B.T.U. (2184 cubic feet multiplied by 4) air-conditioner in the living room, and a 5,000 one (1232 cubic feet multiplied by 4) in the dining room—would be more efficient; however, the cost of purchasing two units is usually quite a bit higher.

If you prefer not to go through determining the volume of your living area that you wish to cool and the average maximum summer temperature, you can use the Room Air Conditioner Sizing Chart—with B.T.U. capacities converted to *square* feet—prepared by the Electrical Industries Association of Southern California and reproduced in the Appendix of this book. However, there is guesswork involved, since the phrase "similar areas" requires some climatologic knowledge.

The most efficient approach to selecting an air-conditioner is to calculate your B.T.U. requirement by using the volume and "cooling factor" described earlier, to check it against the E.I.A. chart in the Appendix, and finally to double-check your findings with the salesman from whom you are planning to purchase your cooling system.

If the salesman tells you that you need 2,000 B.T.U. more than you figured on, the chances are that you are including your kitchen in your "air-space to be cooled," and if that is the case, you do need 2,000 B.T.U. more to counter the heat level of the kitchen area. Knowing that your air-conditioning is of the required capacity, you can start checking the following energy-conserving measures.

1. *The thermostat*. Set it at some point between 75-80° F. and "let it be," as the Beatles put it, until an inordinately hot weather front settles over your area—the so-called "heat wave," during which outside temperatures soar way above 100° F. in the daytime and climb back up there, after a brief descent during the night, every day for several days in a row. When that happens, turn the thermostat setting *down* about five degrees in the late evening, and back up late in the morning (use a timer if there is no one home at that hour), repeating these adjustments for the durtaion of the heat wave. Your house "weathercools" automatically during the night, and in the morning the air-conditioner will have the "cold storage" support of the house to fight off the heat of the day.

2. *Insulation*. Follow the procedure suggested under *Insulation* in the preceding section, *Heating and the Trident Principle*. Everything mentioned—weather stripping, storm windows, shutting the fireplace damper, drawing the drapes (and/or shades and Venetian blinds)—applies to air-conditioner energy conservation.

Since the air-conditioner's arch-enemy is the sun, and since the most vulnerable part of your home to the sun's pounding rays is the roof, you should consider what lies above your head, particularly if your home happens to have an attic or if you live on the top floor of an apartment house. You may very well have an air-conditioning unit working its fan off, so to speak, trying to keep your home cool and comfortable, while at the same time there is a solar furnace between your ceiling and your roof frustrating your cooler's efforts. If you are a renter, consult your landlord. If you are an owner and if there is a direct pasageway between the living area of your home and the attic, via a staircase or a trapdoor in the ceiling, then the air-conditioner is even further overworked (wastefully) in its futile effort to cool an area that is beyond its reach.

Whether the attic is accessible or not from the interior of your home (some attics can be entered only from the outside and are little more than crawl-spaces between the ceiling and the roof), insulating the living-area ceiling from the attic air-space and the latter from the roof, and then providing ventilation for the air in the attic, will cut down on the energy consumption of your air-conditioner to more than an appreciable extent. A thick layer of insulating material should be installed to cover the floor and the ceiling of the attic.

This can be done with relative ease by using either *semirigid* or *flexible* insulation that may be purchased at home-improvement and maintenance centers. Into the first category of these insulation materials fall felts that have some flexibility and are available in panels of different widths, lengths, and thicknesses. Flexible insulation includes rubber or plastic "foams" and quilts and blankets having fabric or paper on each side with loosely packed material between the coverings. Metal foils that are used in crumpled form as filling material or as thin sheets separated by air spaces is another form of flexible insulation.

Fastening either semirigid or flexible insulation to the floor and ceiling of the attic is relatively simple if you use a semiliquid adhesive (such as rubber or plastic cement) and, wherever practical, staples and tacks. Try to butt the panels edge to edge. But if doing so is difficult, don't worry—the overall effect will greatly outweigh the minor imperfections. Having taken care of the floor and ceiling of the attic, and if there is direct access from the interior of the house to the attic, use weather stripping between the door (regular or trap) opening into the living area of the house and the door's enclosing frame.

With the insulation taken care of, it is not likely that you will need forced ventilation in the attic, which involves installation of a regular window-fan large enough to provide an air change in the attic at regular intervals. (Such a fan consumes approximately 270 kilowatt-hours of electricity in one year.) Natural ventilation that the several, usually grated, openings in the attic walls provide should be sufficient. Simply make sure that the grating is not clogged with dirt.

The effort you expended between your ceiling and your roof will decrease the energy consumption not only of your air-conditioning system in the summer months, but of your heating system in winter as well.

3. *Location of air-conditioning unit or units.* The ideal location for the air-conditioner is above the living area that is to be cooled. There are two reasons for this: 1) Cold air has a higher density than hot air (consequently, placing the unit above the ceiling puts gravity to work, decreasing the time required to cool a room); 2) An air-conditioning unit that is located somewhere above is totally out of the way. Placing it on the *roof,* however, contributes very little to either the esthetics of your home or to the unit's efficiency, unless your roof is shaded from the sun, either by trees or other buildings.

If your house has an attic, and if you have insulated that attic, *there* is the ideal spot for the air-conditioner. If your house has a flat-roof construction, or if you live in a condominium apartment where the roof belongs to someone living above you, install your air-conditioner in a shaded location if possible. If not, install it where the rays of the sun spend the least amount of time. Keep it away from areas where excessive outside dust, pollens, or odors will be drawn into it. Clean and replace the filter as often as the manufacturer recommends, regardless of where the unit is located.

4. *Shade.* Draw your drapes, shades, and blinds during the heat of the day to reduce cooling loss. If you have a shade tree on the southwest side of your house, treat it kindly: Its shade in the summer is helping you to conserve energy, and in the winter it tries its best *not* to blot out the sun by shedding its leaves. If you are not thus naturally blessed, consider installing outside awnings, cool shade screens, or bamboo drapes on that side of the house or apartment.

Consider planting a shade tree. A great many nurseries carry an assortment of ready-for-planting, "weaned" trees to suit your individual taste. And, speaking of taste, do not disregard a fruit tree as a possible choice: A lemon tree, for example, will provide your house with the cooling shade that will cut down on your air-conditioner's energy consumption and will supply you with lemons for lemonade. With an apple tree you get shade, nourishing fruit, and cider—just keep an eye out for that machete-swinging doctor next door!

So much for conservation. What about the *second* element of the Trident Principle—*substitution*—as far as cooling the home goes? Is there anything that can be used *instead* of an air-conditioner?

A hand-operated fan is tiring, you say. An electric fan doesn't seem to do anything but blow hot air around. If that has been your experience, try setting it by an open window on the side of the house or apartment which is not getting direct sunlight during the hottest hours of the day. You may discover that the temperature in the room where the fan is drops by as much as ten degrees.

Another, though considerably complicated, approach to cooling your house—and it best be resorted to only if it *is* your house—is the "artificial rain" system, not much unlike that set up in Disneyland's Tiki-Tiki Room. Basically, it consists of a water-storage tank set up where the sun's rays cannot get to it, a water pump, small-diameter water-carrying pipe to deliver water vertically (*up*, at each corner of the house), additional water piping (running horizontally around the eaves of the house and "perforated" along the lowermost side—to "bring down the rain"), and a "gutter" to catch the "rain" and deliver it back to the storage tank.

Unquestionably, this is somewhat of an exotic approach to beating the energy crisis in the home. However, it is worth considering if you are adept with tools. By adjusting the water pressure at the pump, you may be able to vary your rainfall from a drizzle to a downpour—and if you manage to do something not quite right somewhere along the way, your house may wind up being declared a disaster area!

Actually, a more practical substitute for the air-conditioner is your water-sprinkler system. If there is no shortage of water in your area, and if your water bill is reasonable, turning on the sprinklers during the hottest part of the day will cool the area surrounding your house and just might make the summer heat bearable.

For Apartment Dwellers Only

Do not be disheartened by the idea that people who rent, lease, or own houses, as opposed to apartment dwellers, have a greater freedom to conserve energy in that *they* have individual thermostats for both heating and air conditioning that they can control, *they* can make use of the fireplace to cut down on their heating bill, and *their* landlord isn't watching over their shoulder every moment to see what they are going to do with that hammer or screwdriver.

In most cases, the problem of apartment dwellers who do not pay their own utilities bills is less one of conserving energy than of trying to survive through the landlord's conservation methods. If *your* landlord's solution to any energy shortage or upping of the utility rates is to shut the heat off in winter and the air conditioning off in summer, you can do the following:

In winter:

a. Pick up an electric heater or two, preferably with built-in fans to help circulate warmed air.

b. Wear warm clothing—including long underwear —while at home.

c. Buy adhesive-type insulation stripping and install it around window sashes and window frames as well as around any doors where air leakage is noticeable.

d. If there is a ktichen in your apartment, turn on the oven and leave the oven door open; you can do the same with the burners. You might even buy a hot-plate—and use it in the bedroom; both for cooking and for added warmth.

e. If the landlord or manager complains, tell him that the only other alternative you had was to put a complaint about his "conserving methods" to the local utilities commission. If this results in an argument, you will feel considerably warmer at the end of it; the term, "getting all hot and bothered," comes into play here—*you* get hot, and the honorable *landlord* gets bothered.

In summer:

a. Buy a portable air-water cooler if you have to. You can pick one up at a reasonable price (between $20 and $30) at your local drugstore. Fill it with water as required, then place it against a partially open window. It will cool the air in your apartment by about ten degrees and circulate the air.

b. Make yourself at home; strip down to the limit of your inhibitions and fix yourself a cold drink.

c. Take a cold shower at regular intervals.

d. If there is even the slightest breeze outside, open all the windows; this will create a draft and cool your apartment down considerably.

Lighting and the Trident Principle

Conservation. Turning off lights in empty rooms is undoubtedly one of the most efficient ways to cut down on the consumption of electricity. If you happen to have children, you probably know that trying to keep vacant rooms dark can be a frustrating experience. All children—*regardless* of their height—seem to be just tall enough to push the light switch up into the On position, but not tall enough to reach it to bring it back down. Of course, a goodly number of us adults, too, seem to be thus afflicted. And reversing the wiring in the switches will not help. Perhaps, eventually, a "seeingeye" beam will be developed that will automatically switch the lights off when the last person leaves a room.

Until such time, however, we will have to learn to flick the lights off after ourselves and our offspring.

Now let's consider some supplementary methods of conserving our lighting energy.

We know that a 100-watt incandescent light bulb uses the same amount of energy as does a 100-watt fluorescent light. But we may not know *that a 100-watt flourescent light gives off up to three times as much light as does its 100-watt incandescent relative!* For obvious reasons, this is not a fact that your electric utilities company likes to advertise.

But it is a fact that means you can actually increase the amount of lighting in your home by 100% and at the same time cut your electric energy consumption—as well as your utilities bill for electricity

—by 30%! For example, if you replace your 150-watt incandescent light fixture with a 100-watt fluorescent light source, you will be using 50 watts less of electricity but getting up to 300 "incandescent watts worth" *more* light. And conversion from incandescence to fluorescence is neither costly nor difficult. If you know how to operate a screwdriver and a wrench—which, in most instances, is the extent of tools needed—there is no reason why you cannot effect the conversion yourself. *Be sure to disengage the main power switch*, however, before you pick up the tools!

Another method of conserving energy in electric lighting involves nothing more than replacing high-wattage bulbs with those of lower watt-rating. It is as simple a method as any, and for that reason is preferable to conversion to fluorescence wherever a dim light will do as well as a bright one. Your closets, hallways, porches, for example, may be some of the areas that do not require the high-wattage bulbs you have burning there now.

Although both conversion to fluorescence and replacement of bright lights with dimmer ones appears to be an application of the *substitution* principle, strictly speaking it is not since you are still using (though, admittedly, considerably less) electric energy and electric lights. Substitution would involve removing an electric light bulb and substituting something else for it.

Substitution. The trick, here, is "doing it with mirrors." As long as we are *substituting* and not *backtracking*, an electric light source is still necessary. In backtracking, the "mirror trick" is worked with candles, kerosene lamps, whale oil lamps, sunlight in the daytime. (There is a theory that the ancient Egyptians who decorated the walls and ceilings of the burial chambers deep within the pyramids with detailed paintings, did so by bringing sunlight into the darkness of the vaults, by bouncing it off an array of mirrors.)

Basically, there are two types of mirror surfaces you can use to conserve electricity: *flat* mirror surfaces (such as those you have hanging on your dining-room or living-room wall, over your dresser, or over your sink in the bathroom) and *curved* mirror surfaces (which include light-concentrating reflectors used primarily in photo studios and magnifying mirrors).

One of the drawbacks of flat mirror surfaces is that there is but one way in which they will add to the light intensity of the original light source, and that is when they are brought into close proximity of the light source. In other words, if you have a 100-watt light bulb in your dining room and you replace it with a 75-watt bulb, your hanging a mirror on the wall will not only not *double* the light intensity, it will probably not even compensate for the 25 watts that have been sacrificed by the bulb substitution. The only way your 75-watt lamp will give you more light that the original 100-watt one did is if you locate it right next to the mirror surface.

Do not be misled into thinking that 75 watts in the socket and 75 watts in the mirror add up to a total of 150 watts. If you think of illumination as a function of distance, it becomes clear why this is true. Consider the lamp in the mirror as a lamp in an adjacent room, with an opening connecting the two rooms that is the size of the mirror. The closer you bring the lamp to the mirror, the closer you are bringing the light "in the other room" to the room in which you are, which increases the total illumination in the room.

One of the best arrangements in conserving electrictiy by substituting mirrors in place of "lost" light is one where the light bulb is located in a corner formed by mirrors. If you are interested in obtaining more concentrated illumination than overall, diffuse light, the answer lies in curved mirror surfaces. Concentrated light is usually desired over table surfaces, desk tops, and other areas where insufficient lighting may cause eye strain.

Fortunately, you don't have to worry about bending any of your regular mirrors into the most efficient shape or trying to arrange mirror fragments— the frequent end result, as my son found out, of a "bent" mirror. You can purchase curved reflectors practically wherever lighting fixtures are sold or at photo supply stores. Try the lighting fixture department of your nearest dime- or department store first. These reflectors will not give you the intensity of light, in most cases, as will those sold in photo supply stores, but they should be satisfactory for your purposes and are considerably less expensive.

Installing them requires no more mechanical aptitude than screwing in a light bulb. Remember to use a lower wattage bulb than you were using before. The name of the game is beating-the-energy-crisis-in-the-home, and in the case of electric lights you are throwing the problem a curve that will both cut down on your consumption of electricity and at the same time give you more light.

But don't bask in that reflected glory; use it to write letters to your congressman, to the Director of the Ford Foundation's Energy Policy Project, to the Director for Energy and the Environment in the President's Office of Science and Technology, to the Chairman of the Federal Power Commission, to anyone and everyone who should be doing something about the energy crisis. Otherwise we will all have to resort to the third stage of the Trident Principle: *backtracking*.

Backtracking. The generators supplying you and me and all the rest of us have stopped spinning. There's a blackout. It's an unpleasant prospect, true. However, do not panic.

Before there were electric lights, there were gas lights; before gas light there were candles, and oil lamps, and kerosene lamps, and sunlight in the daytime. . . . And man enjoyed life just the same!

Chapter 2

Fun, Food—and Energy

Cooking and the Trident Principle

There are a number of ways in which both the gas and the electric fuel can be conserved in your kitchen. Perhaps one of the most effective, and overlooked, methods involves *timing*. Both a burnt dinner and a cold dinner that requires reheating are examples of off-timing and energy waste. If the burnt dinner is furthermore "burnt to a crisp"—a common-usage term that suggests how common burnt dinners are—there is in addition to the waste of energy the wasting of food.

One of our common human failings is expecting perfection in others—specifically, in fry cooks and chefs in restaurants—and excusing imperfection in ourselves. When we go to a restaurant and order steak, we want it cooked "just right": anywhere from blood-rare to extra-well done. We want it neither charred to the consistency of charcoal nor warmed over.

In our own home, on the other hand, we often find ourselves dispensing with our in-the-restaurant expectations and gastronomical demands. Which would be excusable—after all, we may not be masters of our steak's fate but we are masters of our own house—if it were not so wasteful.

Quite often, it is true, a charred or a cold dinner, which you reheat, winds up that way because of unforeseen circumstances: Your son or daughter returns home early from school, five minutes before you are due to take the roast out of the oven, and tells you that he or she has decided to quit school, or to get married (the next day), and you start smelling smoke before you know what's happened; your company for dinner arrives half an hour late, and you have to warm up to eating temperature your culinary efforts.

In a great many instances, however, smoke signals from the kitchen or cold steaks on plates are the end result of inefficiency. It matters not whether we term that inefficiency poor planning, forgetfulness, thoughtlessness, or carelessness; the final effect winds up being often tasteless and always energy-wasteful.

In the kitchen, use a timer, or timers if you have several things going: simmering, roasting, boiling, frying, broiling. Follow instructions on the recipes. As far as those whom you are preparing to feed at, let's say, six-thirty are concerned, advise them of the fact that if they are not coming through the door by six-forty they will be eating a cool dinner. And keep your word. Before you know it, *they* will be waiting for *dinner*, instead of the other way around.

Even if school and jobs do not all start at the same

time, make it a point that breakfast is going to be a family affair. Frying six or eight eggs does not take any more time than frying two, and it does not take anywhere as much more gas or electricity as when those six eggs are fried two-at-a-time.

If there is food left over after breakfast, or lunch, or dinner, it is a sign that energy in the preparation of that food has been wasted. And, of course, if it is an excess of prepared viands that cannot be saved for the next meal, or the next *day's* meal, it might point to one of the reasons for the food shortage you've been reading about in the papers.

In short, plan your meals. Don't broil seven steaks when you know only five will be eaten. Allow yourself to make an error now and then, but don't make a habit of it.

Turning now from the *heat* energy used directly in the preparation of meals, let's consider the miscellaneous gadgetry found in the kitchen that runs on electricity.

Let's start with the *refrigerator-freezer*. How can you make it use less energy than it has used until now? Undoubtedly, you've noticed that it "starts up" at periodical intervals, hums for a while, then goes silent. It also starts humming almost every time you open its door. The warm air from the kitchen gets inside, triggers the thermostat, and the motor of the refrigerating system begins to "eat watts" until they are transformed into cold temperature.

Try getting everyone at home in the habit of not opening the refrigerator-freezer door any more often, or for any longer periods of time, than necessary.

If you are planning on having ice cream, or mousse, or chilled strawberries for dessert, get whatever it is out of the freezer or refrigerator compartment, give each member of the family who is going to have dessert a serving, and replace the remainder (if there is any) immediately back into the refrigerator or freezer. It is neither necessary nor conducive to family closeness to have each member of the family help himself (or herself), since such a policy involves the opening of the refrigerator that many times more than once. Deciding on a specific time for snacks will further eliminate much of the load with which we overburden our refrigerators.

Never place anything hot or warm into the refrigerator. Let whatever it is cool to room temperature first, *then* set it in the refrigerator. If you are preparing a beverage that is going to be served with ice—iced tea, coffee, lemonade, for example—use a little less water and make up the difference in volume with ice. Let the pitcher stand for a few minutes, or stir the contents, before setting it in the refrigerator.

We are all chronic dial-twisters, lever-operators, and button-pushers; we have this obsession to adjust everything adjustable, continually, whether it needs adjusting or not. If you have a fully automatic refrigerator-freezer, all you have to remember is to turn the unit off before leaving on your vacation. Be sure that you empty it of all perishables, of which—had you planned properly—there should be next to none.

If your refrigerator has a temperature control dial—as most units do—set the control to slightly above the half-way point between "low" and "high." This setting should keep your perishable foodstuffs cold (*not* frozen) in the refrigerator section, and frozen (*not* solidified to the point that you have to hammer-and-chisel your way to those pork chops in the back) in the freezer compartment.

After you have purchased your groceries and have brought them home, separate those items that will go in the refrigerator from those that will not; *then* proceed to put the first items away.

Follow the maintenance procedure outlined in the manufacturer's brochure. Defrost the refrigerator regularly as needed. Brush or vacuum the condenser coils at the bottom or rear of the unit. If you follow these, as well as the preceding suggestions, you may not have to resort to the Trident Principle's second and third solutions: *substituting* an ice box for your gas or electric appliance, *backtracking* to an iceless (because of unavailability of ice) window cooler.

Which brings us to all those other appliances that cover the modern kitchen's walls, clutter counter tops, and are ingeniously concealed in every available nook and cranny. Unquestionably, the refrigerator, the freezer, and the range are *almost* essential ("almost" because there's always the possibility of *backtracking*) and there is a strong argument for the new electric fry pans, griddles, toasters, and coffee percolators in that they are more efficient and economical than a standard gas or electric stove.

But what about the electric blenders/mixers, carving knives, can openers, knife sharpeners, corkscrew "unscrewers," garbage disposers, dishwashers, and—outside the culinary domain—electric pencil sharpeners, toothbrushes, toothpicks, combs, hair dryers, clocks, typewriters, vacuum cleaners, rug shampooers, scissors, and so on, almost ad infinitum?

Time magazine (November 26, 1973) came out with a defense of such contrivances. In "A Kilowatt Counter's Guide to Saving," we were informed that "contrary to much pop sociology, a proliferation of frivolous power gadgets is not to blame [for the fact that "last year the average U.S. household used some 8,000 kw-h., or more than thirteen times as much as in the 1930s"]. An electric toothbrush uses only 0.5 kw-h. of electricity per year. . . . A carving knife . . . 8 kw-h., . . . a garbage disposer . . . 30 kw-h. per year."

Assuming, just for the sake of argument, that only 1% of our population uses an electric toothbrush, a carving knife, and a garbage disposer, we arrive at a figure of close to *81 million kw-h.* of electricity that is consumed by those three gadgets over a year's period. Which is equivalent to what 10,000 average households (using *Time's* figure of 8,000 kw-h. per household) use in a year's time. Or, to put it another way, the energy consumed annually by 1% of our population's use of the electric toothbrush, carving knife, and garbage disposer *would supply an average household with enough electrical energy to last 10,000 years!* Which boils down not to you, me, or our respective neighbor using but a drop out of the ocean, figuratively speaking, but to the close to four billion of us draining the ocean dry.

And how much labor do we *really* save by using many of those power gadgets? Does it take that much effort to raise a "powerless" toothbrush to one's mouth and move it briskly ten or twenty times the distance of one inch than it does to heft a power tool to the same position and then flick a switch? How much labor is expended in operating a manual can opener?

Over a year's span the garbage disposer undoubtedly chews up quite a bit of leftovers. On a daily basis, however, how much work is it to walk your garbage to the trash can? Certainly not enough to give either you or me a hernia. . . .

So, put away those frivolous gadgets. Get some exercise. And conserve that energy. If there is more than one of you in the household, delegate manual labor—taking out the garbage, washing and drying the dishes, operating the manual can opener, etc.—to all members of the family. Switch your responsibilities from one to another on a daily or a weekly basis. You may even get to know one another better, and enjoy each other's company more. It is a form of backtracking that pays emotional as well as practical dividends.

"Moments of crisis produce in men a heightening of life," Chateaubriand wrote a hundred and fifty years ago. The fact that he was writing about the beginning of the revolution in Paris doesn't make that observation any less applicable to the energy crisis in your kitchen.

Entertainment and the Trident Principle

Considering how hard you work—it matters not whether it's laying bricks, sitting at a desk, running around all day, or keeping the house clean—you deserve, and have an absolute right, to have fun. Man has had a social life ever since the day one of our great-great-great-grand-ancestors burned his hand while reaching into the fire to grab a handful of burnt deer, yelled: "[expletive deleted]! That's hot stuff!" made a face while he shook his hand in the typical after-the-burn gesture that has survived with us to this day, and made his common-law cavemate laugh.

If you get right down to it, if you observe our current sources of entertainment with an unbiased, critical eye, the substance of "entertainment" in an overwhelming majority of cases has not really progressed much since that day. The *methods of delivering* entertainment to us have improved beyond even our *recent* predecessors' wildest dreams, but the substance?

Now, be perfectly honest with yourself. What was the last TV program that you really and truly enjoyed? It wasn't *the last one you watched*, was it? If it was, ask yourself that same question six, twelve, eighteen, twenty-four hours from now. You will more than likely discover that your TV-viewing habit is just that—a habit. It is a habit that isn't hard to break, and the breaking of it does not *eliminate* television-viewing, it simply limits it through the utilization of selectivity. *Yours.* Don't let anyone tell you what programs you should watch, but see if you can't cut your in-front-of-the-TV-set presence to one-half what it has (habitually) been.

You will discover that you can, quite easily. It is one habit the breaking of which does not, usually, cause withdrawal pains.

If you succeed, you will conserve 270 kilowatt-hours (average usage as determined by the Citizen's Advisory Committee in Environmental Quality) over a year's time if you have a color-TV set, 200 kw-hrs. if you have a black-and-white set. If those figures do not sound impressive, take the lower of the two—200 kw-hrs.—and multiply it by 18 million, which is *not* the total number of TV sets in the country but is just the most recent circulation figure (rounded off) of *TV Guide.* Conservation by way of *TV Guide* subscribers' selectivity alone would amount to *over three and one-half billion kilowatt-hours,* which is the amount of energy Grand Coulee dam—the largest in the country—takes ten weeks to generate.

All right, you say, *I select the programs, I cut my viewing in half, I give Grand Coulee a rest, but what do I do with that free time?*

Having already made acquaintance with the Trident Principle, you probably have an inkling of what's coming.

Substitution. The alternatives to watching television are limitless. Think of all those things you wanted to do but "never had the time." Let's consider some possibilities in the way of entertainment for a single person, for a couple, and for a family, and in each case let's try to touch upon both the daytime and nighttime leisure periods.

If you are a single person with free evenings, you can:

1. Learn to play a musical instrument.
2. Start a hobby: Star- and planet-gazing can be fascinating even through a low-power, low-cost telescope or high-powered binoculars (the rugged, cratered lunar crescent or disk, Jovian moons, the rings of Saturn, the joyfully brilliant cluster of the Pleiades, the Great North American nebula—a puff of starlight studded with tiny diamonds—in Orion's "dagger," and a multitude of other spectacular displays are within your eye's reach to enjoy). Stamp-collecting, once you begin, may develop into a delightful obsession. So may handicrafts (from crocheting to sculpting), writing, sketching, drawing . . .
3. Try your luck at solitaire, have fun with crossword puzzles.
4. Spend the evening with that friend whom you've meant to see for so long, back in the days when you never "had the time."
5. Go bowling, golfing (there are some night courses), swimming . . .
6. Take an hour's walk and see the city—or country—by moonlight and from a pedestrian's point of view for a change.

If you are a single person with free daylight hours, you can, in addition to any of the above (to the exclusion of star-gazing and seeing the neighborhood by moonlight):

1. Get outdoors and try your hand at painting or drawing scenic pictures.
2. Visit the art museum or the natural museum of science or the planetarium.
3. Go beachcombing, climb over the rocks at low tide and peer closely at the colorful, living world crawling, wavering, swimming in the tidal pools. Or go to the mountains, the forest, the lake, the

stream, the desert—look at the world as you had never looked at it before, and you may realize to your pleasant surprise that you had never seen it before.

If you are a couple, free in the evenings, you can share everything that was suggested for the single in the evening, only in addition to that you can:

1. Talk to each other.

2. Play any one of the many dialogue-prompting games that are on the market, among them: Image, Facts in Five, Mr. President, Landslide, Airport, Ecology, Realm, and Infinity, to list but a few. They range from quite simple to almost maddeningly complex covering an equally broad range of interests—from the romantic to the militaristic. Most of these can be purchased either at large department stores or in book and toy shops; others have to be ordered directly from the manufacturers.

3. Go for a moonlight stroll together.

If you are a couple free in the daytime, don't dismiss any of the suggestions for activities that can be done alone. And in addition try horseback riding, sailing the lake, the river, or the sea, or rowing in the park.

Finally, *if you are family,* try any of the leisure-time activities above—from gazing at the Andromeda galaxy, together, one at a time, at night, to sailing the waters. And top your activities off once in a while by an overnight camping trip to the nearest "wilds." Pack some sleeping bags, and a backpack with provisions for all (take two packs if one won't be sufficient), and backtrack into the wilderness. Reach your initial destination by *economy* car, bus or train.

Always remember: Before there was television, there was radio, before there was radio, there were books and magazines and newspapers and live concerts and plays . . .

Chapter 3

On the Road

In 1894, at the Universal Exhibition in Paris (at which the Eiffel Tower was opened to the public), one of the major attractions was a "curiosity": the first automobile, a Benz. Some car buffs may argue that "the first automobile" was the steam-driven, three-wheeled carriage (introduced in 1769, also in Paris, by Nicolas Joseph Cugnot), or the 1894 gasoline-powered Panhard.

Actually, it doesn't really matter whether the credit for the first "horseless carriage" is given to Germany's Benz or Daimler, to the United States' Morrison, Duryea, Maxim, Kettering or Roper, or to Austria's Marcus. The fact remains that none of the above-mentioned gentlemen could have had the least inkling that within three-quarters of a century the descendants of their brainchildren—in all of their multifarious hybrid forms—would become our indispensible means of transport, our beasts of burden, our status symbols, and our headaches.

Conservation of Fuel Begins in the Showroom or on the Lot

Let's assume that you are seriously thinking of buying a car or of trading in the one you have. One of the first questions you should ask yourself is: Why? It is not at all an unfair question, yet many of us shy away from posing it to ourselves, or when we do pose it we come up with an answer, or set of answers, that either begs the question or, by virtue of the answer's ambiguity, strongly suggests that our reason is more often one of whimsy than of valid need.

There are basically three species of car buyers: 1) the buyer who does *not* have a car and wishes to own one, 2) the buyer who *has* a car and wishes to trade it in, and 3) the buyer who has *one* car and wishes to buy another one.

Assuming that each of the three buyers has given a valid reason for needing *a* car, needing a *new* car, or needing an *additional* car, the chances are that each of the three prospective buyers has his sights set on a certain make and model of car in preference to other makes and models.

And this is where—today more than at any other time in the history of the automobile—you, as the car buyer, should question yourself in regard to your preference. We've all been buying cars for far too long for far too many wrong reasons. Perhaps two of the least important reasons have been style and status symbolism.

The prime function of the automobile is to get us

from here to there within a reasonable amount of time. The time it takes us to get from point A to point B is determined less by the "oodles of power under the hood" than it is by the conditions of the road and by the speed laws of city streets and state and federal highways. Examining the cars we've been buying over the past two decades, it becomes obvious that we have either totally forgotten what cars are for or we have been thoroughly brainwashed by the auto manufacturers' adds. By bombarding us with superlatives of the superfluous, these ads try to convince us that the automobile should be something on the order of an esthetically designed torpedo with bucket seats.

In 1967, Lincoln Continental offered us a "refinement" of "wraparound parking lights and taillights." In 1969, a General Motors ad promoting the 1970 Chevelle SS 396 stated that "the standard V8 has been kicked up to 350 hp." In 1971, Ford announced: "We held a tea party in our Mercury Marquis to show you how smoothly it rides." And in 1973, we were being offered the Capri as "the first sexy European at a shamefully low price."

It wasn't until we found ourselves wrapping around the block for an hour-long wait to get to the gas pump that the words "economy" and "gas mileage" began to crop up in every last automobile ad and commercial, from Honda's to Cadillac's. Which brings us back to the showroom, if you are planning to buy a new car, or to the car lot, if it's a secondhand automobile you are after.

Obviously, the determining factors for your selection of a car should be neither style nor the previously mentioned "status symbolism." Even "riding comfort" or "the smoothness of ride" should be considered as *desirables* rather than *essentials*. After all, your grand-ancestors crossed the prairies in conveyances a lot less comfortable than the least comfortable of today's automotive wonders.

Consider the engine first. And think in terms of gas economy. Then consider the size of the car. Check into the warrantee that is offered. Go over the safety features. Compare the list price of the car with no optional extras with the total list price of the car, including options. Start eliminating options that amount to little more than frill—frill equals additional and unnecessary weight, and additional weight equals lower gas mileage.

Certainly, there is no blanket rule that can be applied for selecting a fuel economy car that meets every individual's and every family's needs. For example, an MG Midget, a Fiat X1/9, or a Honda Civic might be ideal for someone who is never faced with the problem of carrying more than one passenger. But these cars would not be adequate for a family of four.

There is a relatively simple approach you can use, one involving the process of elimination, to arrive at a choice of car that will both conserve fuel and meet your other specifications and requirements.

The approach first and foremost centers on the functional side of the car and on the practical side of car ownership. The matter of style, status symbolism, and even horsepower rating of the engine (if power is an absolute must, consider the diesel) is not considered in any but the most peripheral way.

Let's say you are a family of four and you have been driving a sleek, power-packed, luxurious automobile—a Gas Guzzler Special—which you have decided to trade in for something more rational: an economy car. How do you proceed through the veritable maze of auto manufacturers' claims and counterclaims to the car that's right for you?

Try the following unhurried and orderly approach,

never losing sight of the fact that every car dealer is strongly biased in favor of his particular make of car and is above all else interested in making a sale. That is his *job*. *Your* goal, however, is not to be *sold* a car but to *buy* one—and to buy such a car that will both get you from here to there on the least amount of gas as well as keep you satisfied in matters of size, price, maintenance cost, and safety features. Now start zeroing in on that car:

1. *Select the top-rated ten to twenty economy cars.* Using the most recent gas-mileage figures available from a number of impartial sources (such as the U.S. Environmental Protection Agency, the Consumers Union of the U.S., or any one of the several automotive publications like *Road Test, Car and Driver,* and *Motor Trend)* make a list of the ten to twenty cars that get the best mileage. Do not be satisfied with just one set of figures, however: Gas mileage is a variable that depends on the conditions under which the car was tested, on whether the test car was equipped with manual or automatic transmission, on whether it was the standard model or one that was loaded with options, as well as upon the test driver's driving habits.

Arrange the figures in a list similar to the one reproduced below, noting the extreme disagreement among the testers on some of the makes and models tested. Find out why, for example, the gas mileage obtained by *Motor Trend* magazine was consistently higher (in the case of Fiat 128, exactly *100% higher)* than those obtained by both Consumers Union and Environmental Protection Agency. The following list, by no means complete, shows gas mileages arrived at by Consumer's Union, Environmental Protection Agency, and *Motor Trend.*

| Gas Mileage | | | |
CU	EPA	MT	Automobile Make and Model
31	24.9	35.0	Datsun B210
29	17.4	34.8	Fiat 128
	22.2	34.5	Renault 17
32	27.1	33.9	Toyota Corolla 1200 Coupe
	19.7	32.1	Alfa Romeo 2000 Berlina
	29.1	30.4	Honda Civic
	24.5	30.4	Lotus Europa
25	24.6	30.0	Chevrolet Vega XL
26	22.8		Ford Pinto
26	20.9		Volkswagen Super Beetle
24	18.2		Opel Manta
24	19.4		Saab 99
22	20.1		Ford Mustang II
21	16.7		Ford Maverick

2. *Narrow the list down on the basis of seating capacity.* Of the ten makes and models tested by Consumers Union in the above list, only three were given a "fair" rating for rear sitting comfort: The Saab 99, the Ford Maverick, and the Fiat 128. Check their opinion out. Take the whole family and test drive the Saab, the Maverick, and the Fiat, but don't stop there. Test drive any and all of the others except those that are obviously too small for the four of you to get into without turning into pretzels.

3. *Take a look at the price tags.* In order not to complicate the process, let's assume that you've narrowed the field down to the Saab 99, the Ford Maverick, and the Fiat 128. Let's also assume that you are an average family with an average income and that you do not wish to spend more than $3000 for your new car. Let's disregard the trade-in value of your Gas Guzzler Special, the possible finance charges on the new car, as well as the registration and license fees (these will be discussed in the chap-

ter on how to beat the money shortage). Let's look at the prices and see if the field of choice can be narrowed down even further. (Under the heading, "List Price," for imports, at East Coast point of entry; all prices—subject to change—are for 2-door, 4-cylinder, 4-speed manual transmission models, and include AM radio.)

Make and Model of Car	List Price	Gas Mileage
Fiat 128	$2593	17.4-34.8
Ford Maverick	2919	16.7-21
Saab 99	5153	19.4-24

Now considering your hypothetical budget ceiling, if your eye liked the Saab more than it did the other two competitors for your ownership, drop a lid over your eye and allow yourself to do no more than whisper, "Well, there goes the Saab." If you liked either one of the remaining two cars more than you did the one that got away, then you are saved that bit of theatrical technique.

Look at your narrowed selection of cars—and the chances are that you, your spouse, and your children will disagree as to which of the two finalists (or however many *your* list leaves you with) you like better. Remember: Style and status symbolism are irrelevant. Convince yourself of this and you will have no difficulty making your final choice by studying the important and relevant characteristics each of the remaining cars offers. Compare the safety features, the warrantees, the breakdown potential (mechanical, electrical, hydraulic), and ease of maintenance.

Then, pick the winner and drive off—after you've taken care of the financial arrangements, of course.

Conserving Fuel at and Between Service Stations

Take advantage of the fact that there are at present no lines at the service stations and check your gas mileage with different brands of gasoline. It's the only way you will convince yourself that higher price does not necessarily mean more miles for your dimes or—considering the skyrocketing gasoline prices—for your quarters. Once you've decided on the particular brand of gas that gives you best mileage, check your fuel consumption periodically. Do not be concerned about slight fluctuations in gas mileage which are normal but do start asking questions (of the dealer you bought the car from as well as of your service station operator) if there is a suddenly noticeable downgrading of gas mileage or if there is a gradual trend in that direction. The problem may be mechanical and it may be either in your car or at the oil refinery.

In the event that the wraparound-the-block phenomenon, which we all recently experienced, occurs again—and it might, having been tested and proven to be profitable—you may want to try one of the following maneuvers to lighten the inconvenience of waiting in the long line of irate and impatient motorists inching toward the pumps.

1. Have someone else do the "inching" for you. You may turn to one of the services which, for a fee, will pick up your car and then return it to you full. Or you may want to up your youngsters' weekly allowance in exchange for the identical service. Just be sure they have valid drivers' licenses.

2. Leave your car overnight at your neighborhood station, if there is one within walking distance, after making an arrangement with the operator to have it full and waiting for you in the morning. Most service-station owners, managers, and operators are amenable to this if it doesn't cut into their time.

As a matter of fact, their amenability is directly proportional to *your* amiability, suggesting:

3. Take your neighborhood service-station owner, manager, or operator out for a drink.

4. Marry him. Or his daughter. Let your conscience decide which of the two is the better match.

Now that you have your gas tank full, conserve your fuel. But don't make a fetish out of it. Your sleeping in the trunk of the car to prevent someone from siphoning off your gas tank may be sufficient grounds for divorce. Conserve by simply getting in the habit of relaxed, effortless driving. You will be surprised how much longer that tankful of gas will last and how much more ground you will be able to cover with it if you follow the start-to-finish procedure outlined below.

a. Before getting into the car, check to see if there is anything in it that you will not need on this particular trip—the equipment or baggage in the trunk, for example, or the St. Bernard in the back seat. Be reasonable, of course. Do not insist that your wife stay home if you are moving to a new house.

b. Once in the driver's seat, see if the engine won't start immediately without your touching the gas pedal. If it won't start that way, apply no more pressure to the pedal than is necessary to start the engine. Don't race the engine or pump the accelerator. As long as you are in "neutral" or stopped at a traffic light, you are not moving and if you are not moving your making it *sound* like you are does nothing other than waste gas.

c. When you *are* ready to move do not try to get wherever you are going before you've left. Your car a rabbit is not. Don't try to make it leap.

d. Once your car has started moving, accelerate at an even and gradual pace. If you have a tachometer in your car, and if your car is equipped with manual transmission, shift from gear to gear when the tachometer needle approaches 2500 rpm.

- e. Avoid sudden stops. Try to maintain a steady speed that will carry you through green traffic lights.

f. Out on the highway or freeway, limit your speed to 55 miles per hour. Enjoy the scenery. Relax.

g. Follow the instructions in your owner's manual. Have your car regularly serviced; maintain your tires at the correct pressure; keep the wheels properly aligned.

In addition to the above, map out your trips, eliminating the need to retrace your treadmarks, and avoid turning on your air-conditioner for as long as possible. Use the air vents, stop for a cold drink, slip an ice cube down the back or front of your neck. By the time that ice cube melts you will probably have arrived at your destination.

And your trip probably will have been a more pleasant one than usual.

Alternatives to Driving

1. *Pooling.* Theoretically speaking, two persons using one car to go from point A to point B and back to A will use only 50% of the amount of gas they would use were they to go in two separate cars. Practically speaking, because of the additional weight in the car, they will use *close* to 50% less gas than they would if they traveled in separate cars.

It takes two to pool, and the only requirement is that the poolers live close enough to each other and work for the same or geographically close firms or attend the same school.

Start a "pooling project" where you work or at your school. You may discover that the world is a lot smaller than you'd been led to believe, and considerably more congenial.

2. *Public transit.* Buses, street cars, trains, and

even cable cars may be another alternative to your daily driving. In a great many cases—specifically in those where parking after you get there is a problem—these public means of transportation offer not only relief to frustration and automotive gas pains, but an opportunity to relax before and after work or school, to read, to snooze, to dream. Many metropolitan areas offer excellent public transit systems.

Consider them not only on a day-to-day basis but for your vacation time as well. In addition, Greyhound, Continental Trailways, Amtrak, air lines, steamship lines are all there, ready and waiting for you.

3. *Motorcycling*. Regardless of whether you are a rock-music-loving college student or a reserved parochial-school teacher, the motorized two-wheeled seat with the handlebars to guide you may be your answer. Highly economical (the average bike gets 50 to 60 miles per gallon), these machines come in precision-tuned, low-decibel models that no longer require you to break the sound barrier before you can get away from their roar.

Test drive one. If you have never ridden a motorcycle, start with a smaller one—a 50cc or a 75cc—and progress to the size you feel comfortable on. The price tag varies as it does with automobiles, but the general range is from around $400 for a 75cc to $2000 for a 750cc machine.

If you are planning on using a motorcycle on the highway, make certain that you get one that satisfies the minimum power requirement set by the Department of Motor Vehicles in your state. This minimum varies from state to state. In California, a motorcycle on the freeway with an engine that does not develop the low threshold of 15 horsepower will produce a highway patrolman in your rear-view mirror and a traffic citation.

Although there is a relationship between displacement of an engine (in cubic centimeters) and its power (in horsepower), it varies in value from one make of motorcycle to the next. A rough rating equivalent is 8 to 10 horsepower per 100 cubic centimeters.

If you decide to purchase a motorcycle for a cross-country trek, plan your route, check the minimum power requirement in each of the states you are going to traverse, and then buy the machine that will meet the highest minimum.

Finally, as a safety precaution, wear a crash helmet whenever you are riding, and insist that your passenger does the same.

4. *Electric cars and foot-powered cars.* Battery-powered electric cars are neither new nor are they obsolete. The first American "electric automobile" was built in 1890 and could maintain a speed of 14 miles per hour. The first automobile to exceed the speed of 60 mph was Camille Jenatzy's *La Jamais Contente* ("Never Satisfied"). At the turn of the century, 38% of U.S. automobiles were powered by electricity. In 1912, the peak year of the electric automobile's acceptance, there were almost 34,000 "electrics" registered in the United States. Ironically, it was a battery-powered gadget, the electric self-starter, that contributed to the decline of the "electric's" popularity: The little button replaced the hand crank that was until then used to "start" the car with the internal-combustion engine. From that point on, especially with crude oil spurting out of the ground almost wherever you turned, the electric automobile became an antiquated conversation piece, derided for its heavy and inadequate batteries, its low speed, and its short range.

With the oil wells purportedly running dry, however, the electric car is being seriously considered today as the possible answer to fuel shortage as well as to air and noise pollution. In fact, there is a mass-producer of electric passenger cars in the United States today, and there are better, though more expensive, electric automobiles on the way.

You can buy a battery-powered two-seater, with 12 cubic feet of cargo space, from Sebring-Vanguard, Inc., located in Sebring, Florida. Selling for under $2000, the CityCar has a top speed of 28 miles per hour, a range of 50 miles, and its operating cost is ½ cent per mile. The operating cost comes from your recharging the CityCar's batteries off your household current. The 8- to 10-hour charge required to put the 50-mile range back into the car uses less than a quarter's worth of electricity.

The CityCar does set limitations on our driving exuberance, that's true. But, at the same time, it cuts our gasoline consumption to zero, eliminates our contribution to smog, and offers us a promise of better electric cars to come. According to the president of Sebring-Vanguard, Robert G. Beaumont, the company is about to double the CityCar's range by the development of a new battery with better energy-storage capabilities.

Optimistically, Sebring-Vanguard, though the only firm already mass-producing the electric car, is not the only company working on it. Mercedes Benz has developed an experimental electric van (the LE 306 Electro-Transporter) with a top speed of 50 miles per hour, a range of 30 to 60 miles, a payload capacity of one ton, and a "quick change," 144-volt "power plant." Saab is already selling a delivery van powered by batteries with a lifetime of two years and a motor that is expected to last 400,000 miles or 15 years. Westinghouse is another corporation with an electric car in the works.

As Jenifer Harvey puts it, in "Look, Ma, No Gas!

The Electric Car" (*Family Circle*, May 1974): "If the country's 20-million short-trip vehicles and a vast number of delivery vans and types of trucks were replaced by EV's [electrical vehicles], and if there were a gradual change to nuclear [or solar] power generation, we could go a long way toward helping solve the energy crisis."

So consider the silent, gasless car with the extension cord as another possible substitute for your Gas Guzzler Special.

Finally, there is another vehicle on the market you might want to consider: Its makers, Antares Engineering, call it the PPV—People Powered Vehicle. It seats two, is ideal for short trips, uses no gasoline, needs no recharging, is light enough for two people to carry (if such a peculiar need ever arises), goes as fast as your feet can make it go, and it sells for around $350. If you are athletically inclined, you'll love it; if you are not, the exercise will do you good. If you hate exercising, or if you are approaching the age of 85 and feel that you've exercised enough in your lifetime, Antares Engineering offers a model with a small electric motor and a transmission to their three-wheeled marvel.

The Last Word on Locomotion: Backtracking

One of the fail-safe characteristics of the Trident Principle is its built-in promise of another, and yet another ace in the hole. It guarantees that each of its three problem-solving parts (conservation, substitution, and backtracking), *if followed to the letter by all concerned,* will be self-sufficient. Thus, a conscientious and determined effort at conservation of fuel, combined with simultaneous production and neodevelopment, should be adequate. In turn, it is all but inconceivable that the methods of substitution discussed on the preceding pages would not solve the on-the-road energy crisis, were you and I and every other licensed driver in the country to select any one of the methods. However, even if substitution failed, we'd still be able to backtrack.

Many of us engage in what might be called "locomotive backtracking" on and off without ever being conscious of the fact that that is what we are doing. If we do not take conservation of gasoline seriously, we will have no choice but to substitute. If we do not conserve, produce, and neodevelop in the substitution stage, we may run out of the raw materials necessary for the production of substitutes for the gasoline-powered automobile, and will have to backtrack. In the reverse historical order, backtracking would lead us to sailing, paddling, swimming, bicycling, horseback riding, walking.

PART TWO

Beating The Food Shortage

Meat may soon be rivaling sex as a source of jokes. Samples: "Where can I rent a steak?" Or: "I would like to invest in a piece of meat." Vice President Agnew offered his contribution last week: "Two Swiss steaks opened a bank account in Zurich."

—*Time* (April 9, 1973)

In actions dolefully reminiscent of dumping milk and killing little pigs during the Depression, U.S. chicken farmers and cattle raisers last week . . . cut their losses by systematically gassing, drowning and suffocating a million baby chicks and selling their egg-laying hens . . . sent pregnant

sows to the slaughterhouse and dispatched old
milk sows to hamburger heaven. These tactics
raise a two-headed specter of shortages and
higher prices for milk, eggs and meat in the next
few months.

—*Newsweek* (August 6, 1973)

In Los Angeles, a housewife loads her shopping
cart with 100 cans of tuna and returns the follow-
ing day to buy 100 more. Midwestern appliance
makers report soaring freezer sales to consum-
ers who want to stock up with food. Some super-
markets limit the amount of pork and poultry
their customers can purchase. In New York City,
shoppers literally storm a discount food ware-
house and buy up everything in sight.

—*Newsweek* (August 6, 1973)

Within the next five years, a number of the most
important fish species on the Atlantic and Pacific
coasts of the United States may, for all practical
purposes, disappear. . . .

—Robert H. Boyle,
"At the Rate We're Going,
It's Good-by, Fish,"
—*The Reader's Digest* (January, 1974)

Packing houses, some of them chock full of meat
they could not ship to their customers, were
closing down, pulling out of the livestock markets.
Families in some areas were finding short
supplies in the stores, not only of meats but also
of fresh produce.

—*U.S. News & World Report*
(February 18, 1974)

Chapter 4

When Supermarket Shelves Go Bare

Until meat, poultry, bread, milk, toilet paper, and an assortment of other staples suddenly vanished, though temporarily, in 1973, or dwindled to a bare fraction of the quantity in which they had been available previously, the idea of shortages at the supermarket level seemed entirely inconceivable to most of us.

My wife refused to believe that the reason I didn't bring home a package of ground beef from one of the major chain supermarkets—at which she had asked me to stop one day on the way home from work—was because there was no beef, ground or otherwise, and very little pork at the meat counter. As a matter of fact, of the ten specific items she had asked me to get that day, I could only find four. We happen to live in the second most populous metropolitan area in the country.

An unprecedented occurrence? Not at all. Portents of "Soylent Green"? Not necessarily. Those of us who have lived through the days following the Wall Street Crash of 1929 have seen considerably worse times, times of acute nationwide unemployment, of evictions, of bread lines. Some reputable economists are seeing a parallel between the postwar years of the late twenties and the economic and political trends of the seventies. Whether they are right or wrong, the fact remains that the world we are living in today is incalculably more complex than it was at the time of the Depression. To take just one facet of this complexity, a facet directly related to the question of the bare shelves at the supermarket, the population of the United States in 1930 was almost 123 million; today it is close to 204 million. The supermarkets, in other words, have some 80 million more mouths to feed.

On the world front, population has likewise increased—*doubled* since 1930—by a staggering total of 2 *billion* souls (or mouths). The complex intricacy of the worldwide economic network required to maintain a supply-and-demand balance between (and among) the producers and consumers should be appreciated by anyone who's tried to balance his income and expenses without having to worry about the political trends of his neighbors, the crop failure on the next block, the famine across the street, or the price of pork bellies on the stock market.

Considering the situation in other parts of the world—the recent starvation of people in Nigeria, the drought in Africa, the war in the Middle East—our national agricultural and international trade machinery has managed commendably to keep us supplied, for a price, with an extremely wide variety of foodstuffs and commodities. And it is within the phrase "extremely wide variety" that we find a key—substitution—to surviving any unforeseen shortages.

Recent food shortages have been of a sporadic variety. Chasms in the shelf areas shifted from the meat counter to the dairy section, from the canned goods to the fresh produce, from frozen foods to the bakery shelf. And although there have been brief periods of what may be termed "generic" shortages—of beef, for example—most shortages were of the brand-name category. Since, understandably, generic shortages are the kind that create the greatest hardship, let's see how they can be avoided by making use of the conservation phase of the Trident Principle.

Conservation at the Supermarket

A great many of us have been spoiled by our high standard of living and by what we have self-deceptively considered the limitless availability of foods to tickle our palates and please our eyes. George Herbert, one of the English metaphysical poets of the seventeenth century, remarked that "the eye is bigger than the belly." The cuts of steak, the mass of hamburger, or the quantity of fresh produce that we buy, topped in the end by the excess of leftovers we push away to feed the garbage disposer or the trash can, supports Herbert's view. Furthermore, very few of us—in spite of the numerous nutrition guides that are available—make a conscious effort to plan nutritious meals. Too often we equate quantity with nutrition. As a result, we find ourselves much more often stuffed than nourished, and too soon hungry after that.

One of the major disadvantages—one could almost call it a built-in wastage mechanism—of the average supermarket is its prepackaging element. From the fresh meat counter to the frozen foods section, you are faced with packaged portions. The butcher at the supermarket cuts x number of steaks, or pork chops, or veal cutlets, and packages these up to be sold to the consumer. There may be three thick chops in one package, six thinner ones in another, four in the third.

A frozen foods manufacturer—let's say of halibut steaks—makes an even greater effort to have a certain fixed number of equal portions in each package.

Both the butcher and the frozen foods manufacturer totally disregard the fact that a serving or a portion for one person may be two servings for another. And it is beyond reason to expect them to come up with an assortment of packaged meats or poultry or fish labeled, for example: Serves Three, a Boy of 8, a Very Active Male of 37, and a Moderately Active Female of 32.

To conserve you must get away from prepackaged foods, especially if your family is made up of a heterogeneous assortment of individuals, each of whom requires a different caloric and protein intake. Also, you must have a fairly good idea of the caloric and protein content of various foods and the daily requirement for each member of your family. Complete tables listing the nutritive value of foods (in kilocalories, protein, carbohydrates, etc.), as well as the daily intake requirements for males and females of all ages engaged in a wide range of activities, are available at health-food stores, drugstores, supermarkets, and bookstores. Tables of the nutrient content and energy value of some common foods and of the recommended daily intake of nutrients and energy are included in the Appendix of this book.

To illustrate how such knowledge and preplanning results in conservation at the supermarket, let's take a hypothetical family made up of a 42-year-old male who is employed as a construction worker (very active), his 37-year-old mate who works as a receptionist (semisedentary), their six-year-old son, and a daughter of 15.

Checking the recommended daily intake of energy and nutrients table (see Appendix) offers us the following figures: The 42-year-old man requires 3600 calories a day and 90 grams of protein; his wife requires 2150 calories and 54 grams of protein; his daughter, 2300 calories and 58 grams of protein; his son, 1800 calories and 55 grams protein.

Without going into any further detail, it is obvious that a package of four portions or servings of *whatever* is going to result in wastage of food.

Dietetics, the science or art of applying the principles of nutrition to feeding, can be an extremely involved approach to the simple art of eating. However, if one at least applies it in the general sense, the chances are that the practice will serve a dual purpose: It will help you conserve at the supermarket and it will provide you and your family with the nourishment you need.

If you have a fairly large freezer in your home, your best approach to conservation while shopping is to buy meats, fish, poultry, and other perishables in bulk. Some of these purchases may have to be done at specialty shops. If the butcher at your local supermarket will not cut to specifications (*yours*), see if there isn't an independent butcher shop in which you will get this kind of service. Once you get the fresh meat home, portion it out for each member of the family, using a scale, into "meal packages" that are *not* made up of identically sized cuts. Then wrap these separately and freeze. An even better approach would be to wrap the individual portions separately, enabling you to prepare meals only for those who are going to be home to eat them. If the children, for example, are spending a night with their friends, *their* portions will remain frozen until the next night.

The above procedure is not hoarding—it is conservation through prudent planning.

Substitution at the Supermarket

Whereas conservation is an exclusively preventive measure to counteract shortages, substitution is both a preventive step and a remedy when there actually is an unavailability of something.

Having an energy value and nutrient content table again is essential. It will enable you not only to substitute one cut of meat for another, but will offer you limitless alternates to items of food that fall victim of a generic shortage. All of such tables specify the carbohydrate content of each food item, which is information you should specifically pay attention to if you have been prescribed a low-carbohydrate diet.

One of the first habits you should break yourself of is the habit of being brand-conscious. It will temper your feelings of panic in the event that your favorite brand disappears. Remember that almost every item sold at your local supermarket has to—and does—meet with the Food and Drug Administration's approval.

Matters of taste, of course, fall outside any measurable standard, so you cannot depend on the FDA for that criterion. However, adding a pinch of salt or a dash of pepper or other spices will in most cases improve the taste considerably and lead it in whatever direction you wish it to be led.

So substitute. Substitute one cut of meat for another: inside chuck roll for chuck tender, sirloin roast for sirloin steak, blade chop for rib chop. Substitute pork for beef or beef for veal, poultry for pork and fish for poultry. The following groupings of beef cuts are closely related to each cut within each group:

1. Inside chuck roll, chuck tender, blade pot roast or steak, boneless shoulder pot roast or steak, chuck short ribs, petite steak, arm pot roast or steak, and English or Boston cut.

2. Standing rib roast, rib steak, boneless rib steak, and Delmonico or rib eye roast or steak.

3. Club steak, T-bone steak, porterhouse steak, top loin steak, filet mignon tenderloin steak.

4. Pin bone sirloin steak, flat bone sirloin steak, wedge bone and boneless sirloin steaks.

5. Round and top round steaks, standing rump and rolled rump, bottom round steak or pot roast, and eye and heel of round.

6. Shank cross cuts, beef for stew, and fresh and corned brisket.

7. Short ribs, rolled plate, skirt steak fillets and plate beef.

8. Flank steak and flank steak fillets.

9. Tip steak, sirloin tip, and cube steak.

Remember that recipes are not sacred, in spite of what cordon bleus and gourmets say. Forget the meat-cutter's and gastronome's terms for the some forty-plus retail cuts of pork; regard it simply as meat, either fatty or lean, and go from there concocting your own recipes with the ingredients that are available.

It's true that many people are particular about the meats or vegetables they eat, some have religious customs that prohibit their eating certain meats or may be actually revolted at the thought of eating offal, guinea pigs, locusts, snakes, snails, frogs, lizards, dogs, and monkeys. By no means is it suggested that you substitute lizard-snaring for supermarket shopping; do, however, consider the alternatives available at the store. Experiment, diversify your meals, broaden your tastes.

Once in the habit of switching from one staple food to another, or substituting ingredients in recipes, you will not be caught short by any shortage.

Dairy products? Buy fresh milk today, powdered the next, canned the day after that. Try goat's milk. If you develop a taste for it, and if the situation at the dairy counter threatens to become intolerably bleak, you may wind up thinking of buying a goat. It's an animal that's much more compact than a cow, will eat practically anything—including your books, lawn, and the laundry on the line—and makes an excellent, though extremely malodorous, pet. If you feel adventurous enough to invest in a goat for dairy purposes, make certain that it is a goat of the proper gender.

Break away from the American cheese habit; try some of the other cheeses so that you will know which substitute you like best when, and if, the time of cheese reckoning comes. Try using yogurt in place of sour cream or cottage cheese. Yogurt blintzes? Might be the recipe for peace in the Middle East.

Frozen foods and canned goods? Alternate brand names. When the ingredients are available fresh, try duplicating the contents of your favorite frozen food package or can; when all of the ingredients are *not* available, substitute other ingredients.

Fresh produce? Never forgetting the nutritive values of foods, substitute: carrots for lettuce, corn for beans, pineapple for blueberries. Combine what is available into exotic salads you've never heard of, then give them a name. *Enjoy* the creativity that shortages inspire!

Household items, paper goods, detergents? Probably in no other area have we been as much brainwashed by the barrage of commercials fired at us via the TV screens in our living rooms, the billboards, and the newspaper and magazine ads. There are "degreasers," there are "detergents that really clean," there are paper towels "that absorb more," there are shampoos and bubble baths and cheese knives and potato peelers and damp mops and no-stick cooking pans and shaving creams, hot and cold. . . .

Remember when a bar of soap washed a pair of hands and a face in the morning, dishes and floors and clothes and pets during the day, provided lather for shaving and washing hair as well as soap suds for bathing? True, going back to a simple bar of soap would be backtracking, but then—so what? It would not mean you'd have to wash dishes and clothes by hand. Shred the bar of soap on a vegetable shredder, using the fine-shredding side of the tool, and then proceed as you normally would. If you find that the soap flakes or swirls tend to stick to each other or adhere to the shredder, place the bar of soap in the freezer for an hour or so having wrapped it first in plastic or aluminum foil.

Undoubtedly you will discover that you can do as well by substituting in a great many other cases involving detergents, paper goods, and household items you haven't been able to do without—until now.

Chapter 5

Growing Your Own Vegetables

To most of us who have been accustomed to, if not enamored of, the concrete of city dwelling or the non-functional esthetics of suburban landscaping, the mention of vegetable gardening brings to mind an image of a farmhand, a potato patch perhaps, and unsightly fingernails. We think of vegetables as ingredients for salads, for prepared and frozen food packages we purchase at the grocery store, as produce overflowing the bins at the supermarket. Indeed some of us look upon vegetables as being less grown than *manufactured!*

I overheard a young boy perhaps five years old, asking his mother at the supermarket if she would take him "to the factory where they made strawberries." The boy's mother did not help the youngster much by telling him "they didn't allow people there."

Although I didn't quite understand the woman's reply to the child's question, inhaling, and looking at the plastic-covered baskets of strawberries, the pyramids of "waxed" apples and pears and citrus fruit, and then picking up an artificially textured, waxy surfaced cucumber, I understood quite well the boy's impression that the multicolored display in the produce section of the supermarket was synthetically manufactured. There was no aroma there to indicate *life*. And the few individually wrapped items in a bin set apart—half a dozen cucumbers, three or four tomatoes—priced four times higher than those massed in other bins, and tagged "Organically Grown," underlined the fact that we have been for a long time living with a shortage of legitimate, fresh produce.

You may quote Roger Miller and say that "you can't rollerskate in a buffalo herd," and most people will be tempted to agree with you—although I can't see why you can't if you're a buffalo—but you *can* grow your own vegetable garden. And it matters not a bit whether you live on the farm, in a suburban home, or in a city condominium.

If you live on the farm, the chances are you already have a vegetable garden and know all about it.

If you live in a house—suburb or city—and have a backyard, you more than likely have enough ground to get into raising an asortment of vegetables that will keep your salad bowl full most of the year. The initial cost is minimal, and the labor—if such a harsh term may be applied to a pleasant and productive pastime—is highly satisfying in more ways than one. You grow your own food, and you save money. Most of the common vegetables can be planted and harvested within a broad range of dates—from mid-February (earliest planting time for spinach) to the end of November (late harvesting time for Brussels sprouts)—so you do need to depend on, or worry about, precise climatic conditions to obtain excellent results.

Although it is recommended that you follow the instructions on seed packages, the following basic planting and harvesting information for fifteen or so vegetables is applicable to most sections of the country that are not beset by extreme variations in weather and temperature.

Mid-February through March: Planting time for *spinach*. A striplet of land about ten feet long and a foot wide will yield you about twenty spinach plants within 50 days of planting. Harvesting time would then be somewhere between the second week of April and the third week of June.

Try planting seeds at two-day intervals, so that you will have a *harvesting range* of time over which you will have ripe, but never overripe, produce for the table. In other words, if you plant twenty spinach plants in the above one-by-ten strip of ground at two-day intervals, you will be ready for your first harvest of spinach about ten days after you plant the last seeds, and from that day on for the next month and a half have a fresh spinach plant every other day.

In mid-July you can start planting spinach again, preferably in an adjacent striplet of land. The cost of seeds, incidentally, for the twenty plants should be somewhere in the neighborhood of 40 cents, or about one-tenth of what buying the same amount of spinach would cost you at the market.

March: Planting time for *broccoli*. You'll need a wider strip of ground here. A *two*-by-ten foot area of ground will reward you with six broccoli plants for a seed cost of about 80 cents—still about a tenth of what the broccoli would cost you at the grocery store —and a time lapse period of a month to 80 days.

Figure that your broccoli will be ready for the table during the months of May and June. Here again—and with the vegetables which follow—try the scatter-planting method to get the best to the table without having to store it.

March through mid-April: Cabbages and *peas.* Fifty cents worth of cabbage seeds will yield you ten heads of cabbage on a striplet of land equivalent in size used for broccoli (2' by 10'). Harvesting time will take about 70 days, so that mid-May to the end of July will be the time for cabbage picking. You can plant it again during the first three weeks of July. However, it will take over three months before your cabbages are ready during this late planting—figure on the second half of October.

Another 2' by 10' strip of ground is sufficient in size to reward you with *sixty pea plants,* at a cost of a penny a plant. And pea-picking time will coincide with your broccoli harvest, stretching across the months of May and June.

March through April, if you decide on raising your own vegetables, will be your most active months. (Incidentally, *all* of the vegetables that we are talking about here will require a total area that is slightly larger than the area of an average one car garage, 10' by 20'.)

Plant *beets* on a strip of land one foot wide and ten feet long. Fifty cents worth of seeds will yield you $10 worth of beets—fifty of them—that will be ready for harvesting through the months of May and June.

The same area of ground will yield you thirty *leeks,* which will be ready for harvesting from the middle of July to the end of October.

Loose-leaf *lettuce,* with its brief growing time, will be ready for the table from mid-April to the end of June, at which time (from July to mid-August) you can plant another 50 cents worth of lettuce seeds to yield you twenty more heads of lettuce from mid-August to the end of October. A foot and a half to two-foot wide strip of ground will be more than sufficient for this.

If you think you will be able to use about 120 *onions* from mid-June to the end of October, which you can raise on a one-by-ten foot strip of ground, go ahead and use the whole strip. The seeds will cost you about $1.60. If the thought of ten dozen onions makes you want to cry, use a five-foot length strip of ground, cutting your yield as well as your tears in half.

Use the other five feet of ground to plant *parsley*. You should be able to get about thirty parsley plants from that half-strip of land at a cost of about 70 cents. The same amount of parsley purchased at the store would cost you close to $20. Harvesting time will be from June to the end of October.

A foot-and-a-half width of ground will yield you twenty *Swiss chard plants*. The seeds shouldn't cost you more than a quarter, and at the price of Swiss chard at the market you will be saving close to $25! It will be ready for harvesting in May and, if you plant another crop during the months of June and July, you will have Swiss chard on hand through the end of November.

In *April*, plant *carrots*. Then again in July. Harvest the first crop in mid-June through July, the second from mid-September to mid-October. You'll get sixty carrots from a one-by-ten foot strip of ground per planting at a cost of about 45 cents.

In *May*, get the *tomato* seedlings. Follow the instructions on the seed package for bracing the plants to keep the fruit off the ground. The savings here are enormous, relatively speaking, considering the price of this vegetable on the market. A five-by-ten foot strip of ground will yield you about fourteen staked tomato plants, with the value of the produce approaching $80, *at a cost of no more than $21!* Be prepared to harvest the crop from mid-July to the end of September, making sure to scatter-plant the seedlings over the month-long planting time.

May through June: Plant *cucumbers, bush beans,* and *zucchini.*

Use a two-by-ten foot strip of ground for cucumbers. For about 35 cents you will get $20 worth of vegetables from about six plants. Harvest it from July through September.

Eighty-five cents worth of bush bean seeds on a slightly narrower strip of ground will produce sixty plants ready for harvesting in July and August. You can plant a second crop while you are harvesting the first for picking in August and September.

A four-foot wide strip of ground and a dollar's worth of zucchini seeds will result in a dozen zucchini plants, worth close to $80, that will be ready for the table in July, August, and September.

The above is but a sampling of what you can do with a plot of land measuring 10' by 20'. You may want to plant other vegetables than those discussed above, or you may want to use a smaller (or larger) sector of your garden or backyard for your vegetable garden. The "striplets" of usable ground need not be localized in one area. As a matter of fact, in some cases it is even better if you have several small areas that may be used for planting vegetables than one large one. Some plants require more sunlight than others; consequently, an area by a fence that gets sunlight only in the morning or the afternoon might be better for such plants as radishes and carrots, whereas an open area that gets sunlight most of the day is best utilized with plantings of tomatoes, green peppers, and eggplant. Generally speaking, if the vegetable grows underground it can do with less sunlight than the one that grows aboveground.

Do follow instructions on the seed packages, however, to get the most out of your gardening efforts. Water your plants regularly as required, but do not get carried away—too much water forces growth and cuts down on the fruit produced.

If you live in a condominium or a city apartment where the only soil that meets the eye is where the sidewalks crack, do not for a moment feel that you are out of luck as far as raising your own vegetables goes. After all, there are such things as flowerpots and window boxes. And as Alice Skelsey points out in the March, 1973, issue of *Family Circle,* "A packet of seeds, a pot of soil, a spot of sunshine—that's all you need to become a city farmer."

The potentialities of this approach to growing your own vegetable garden are meticulously detailed by Alice Skelsey and her article is highly recommended to anyone who has had an urge to try the green-thumb route yet had been discouraged by the absence of a garden. By utilizing a balcony, a porch, a windowsill, you can expand your flowerpot vegetable garden to a point where you may not have to worry about the shortage of fresh produce at your local supermarket.

Basically, to get best results, choose a nonporous flowerpot or window box for each of the plantings, but be sure that it is provided with drainage holes in the bottom. Use either packaged artificial soils available at every nursery and in some supermarkets or take a trip out to the country, stop at a farm, and ask the owner if you can use some of his soil to fill your flowerpots with. More than likely he will not mind and will not charge you anything, and if he does charge, you will discover that the soil transplanted from a farm to your vegetable garden is, indeed, dirt cheap.

For planting seeds, follow package instructions, and as a rule plant twice as many seeds as the number of plants you wish to wind up with. Make sure the plants get adequate light and "plant food." Since it is not likely that you will want to use natural fertilizer, either in the condominium flowerpot garden or the outdoor variety, buy the potassium, phosophorus, and nitrogen compounds. Most vegetable seed packages specify the type of plant food that is best suited for the specific vegetable that you are planting.

Finally, water each flowerpot and window box adequately and watch the beginning of your vegetable garden's birth as the tiny sprouts start pushing the soil aside, reach for the sun, form leaves, then start miraculously to transform the nutrients in the soil of the flowerpot into cucumbers, tomatoes, carrots, lettuce, or into any of your other favorite vegetables.

Your friends will not fail to comment on the tastiness and crispness of your vegetables, and you may in the end decide that horticulture is not a farmhand, a potato patch, and unsightly fingernails after all.

Chapter 6

Cooking Wisely

In addition to conserving fuel in the kitchen, substituting the heat in the fireplace for the heat at the range, taking the Trident Principle with you to the supermarket and making it work there, and backtracking into growing your own vegetable garden, there are several other steps you can take to anticipate, counter, and even eliminate shortages in the process of preparing your meals.

(Incidentally, hunting and fishing are both applications of the backtracking solution when used to supplement or replace meat and fish normally purchased from public outlets. Obviously, however, such solutions are not practical for the city or the suburbia dweller. Of course, if you are not tied to metropolitan living, if you live within easy access to a wild game habitat or fishing area, you may want to consider backtracking in that direction within the limits imposed by your Fish and Wildlife Service regulations. But don't let the concept of conservation of wildlife, even as you are squeezing the trigger or pulling in the line or the net, ever slip from your mind. Hunting and fishing should not be considered as a sport. Killing or fishing for food is not a sport—and there is seldom any other justifiable reason for either.)

A habit of on-the-spot, conscious improvisation combined with forethought while you are preparing a preplanned meal is one of the most efficient shortage squelchers you can develop.

Let's start with breakfast.

For the majority of people in our society, breakfast consists of one of the following combinations of food, preceded by orange juice (too often not fresh):

a. Eggs (fried, boiled, or poached), meat (ham, bacon sausage, or steak), toast, coffee.

b. Pancakes, or waffles, and coffee.

c. Hot or cold (packaged) cereals with milk, and coffee.

d. Sweet rolls and coffee.

e. Coffee.

If your breakfast consists of the a-group combination, and if you like your eggs fried (in whatever form), fry or grill the meat first, then use the fats left from it to fry the eggs in. If you use a Teflon pan or griddle and do not need grease to fry the eggs in, pour the fats off into a jar and label it with the type of fats it will store (pork, beef, lamb, chicken, etc.). If you make this a habit, you will never notice any shortage of cooking oils, since you will have an ever-ready supply of your own that you will be constantly replenishing.

If you like your eggs scrambled, add half a cup of

milk for every three eggs, and subtract an egg for every cup of milk you add. Thus, if you've been scrambling half a dozen eggs (for two or three people), you need scramble only five, since the cup of milk will both make up for the difference and make the eggs considerably more fluffy to boot. You can use dried or powdered milk (mix five tablespoons of powdered milk in three-quarters of a cup of water). Mixed with eggs, dried or powdered milk is indistinguishable from the liquid kind.

Consider baking the eggs in the oven. By doing this, you will be able to use the oven at the same time for making toast. Butter the top of the bread slices. To prevent drying out, set the temperature in the oven at about 425°; use the upper shelf for the toast, the lower for the eggs.

You can boil or poach your eggs, if you drink instant coffee or tea, in the water you are boiling for your beverage. Use a deep pan; wash the eggs off under hot water in the sink for boiling, then lower them as you normally do into the pan. To poach, crack an egg apiece into a plastic Baggie, twist a tie-lock slightly above the egg, wait for the water to come to a boil, then lower the eggs into the pan. When they are done, scoop them out, cut the Baggie open and spoon the poached egg out. If you have egg holders, set egg and Baggie into each holder, cut the plastic bag about an inch above the egg, fold the plastic down over the egg holder and go to it. When your eggs are cooked, the water will be ready for your tea or coffee.

Whether you've made ham, bacon, sausage, or steak, serve all of the meat on a separate platter. If it's sausage or steak, cut into bite-sized pieces or larger. That way everyone at the breakfast table will help himself to however much each person wants, and there won't be any leftovers that you will have to throw away, because you are going to use all the meat that is left to make your own catchall and unpredictable, but eminently eatable, soup.

Fill a large pot half full with water, set it on the range out of the way, and add all those nutritious leftovers you've been throwing away. Cover it, and let it simmer while you are preparing lunch and dinner. Turn the flame off when you are through in the kitchen. Within two or three days, try what you've concocted. Add some spices to taste. One of the frustrating points about this type of recipeless dish is that it can never be duplicated. But chances are the next potful is going to be even better than the first.

If your choice for breakfast is pancakes or waffles, make your own batter. It takes no longer, costs less, and tastes better. Try to keep about ten pounds of flour, five pounds of sugar, and three dozen eggs on hand at all times. A large can or carton of dried milk will likewise come in handy whenever the recipe calls for regular milk. Use your "sausage"-labeled jar of fats for cooking the pancakes or griddle cakes if you are going to have sausage with them, otherwise use corn oil or margarine. If you prefer butter, and if butter is available, buy it by the pound or more. It's cheaper in larger bulk and can be kept indefinitely frozen.

See if you can break the packaged cold-cereal habit, by preparing your own mixes. It costs less that way, is more nutritious, and much more tasty. Stock up on brown sugar, rolled oats, sunflower seeds, honey, an assortment of nuts, finely ground, raisins, raw wheat germ, and your favorite fruit. Try a combination of rolled oats and/or raw wheat germ with any two of the other staples, pour milk over the mixture, and spoon it up. You may decide from that moment on to bypass forever the prepackaged dry cereal aisle at your supermarket.

Finally, if there is a time shortage in the morning —a shortage which, if habitual, you may try to eliminate by setting the time on your alarm clock fifteen minutes ahead and the alarm fifteen minutes back— crack an egg yolk into a glass (save the egg whites; you never know when a recipe may call for them), add a couple of teaspoons of honey, a dash or two of nutmeg and cinnamon, pour in hot or cold milk (or add five tablespoons of dried milk and use hot or cold water), and stir like crazy before you drink it and dash out the door.

If you are eating lunch at home—which is unlikely if you are employed because of the absurd distances most of us have to cover between home and work— have a bowl of your special soup off the back burner of the range.

If you normally have your lunch at the office, take a thermos of the soup to work with you. For a side dish, fix yourself a fresh vegetable salad with two or three vegetables picked in the morning from your garden.

For dinner, take a steak out of the freezer and figure out how you can feed four with it. Say it's a steak that's just large enough to feed one—if it were prepared and served as steak. How do you extend it into a meal for four? Perhaps if you think of the Chinese, the Melanesians, the Polynesians, and Campbell Soup Company, the answer will come to you: Use the steak as an ingredient and taste teaser in a combination of vegetables or with a pasta, or a cereal, such as rice, buckwheat, barley, millet, or wheat. If you are not using a recipe, there is no telling what kind of an exotic main course you may wind up with. If you *are* using a recipe, and if it calls for ingredients that you do not have on hand, substitute.

Let's say you have the steak out of the freezer and thawing out and you open your recipe or cook book at random to the following: "BAKED SEAFOOD-RICE SALAD."

Normally, of course, you would try to find a recipe for *meat*, and then, wherever necessary, substitute an ingredient here and there if your cupboard or freezer failed to provide those items called for. Just to prove to yourself, however, to what extent substitution will work, go ahead and *bake* yourself a Seafood-Rice Salad, using steak—and, perhaps, a can of tuna—in place of the crab meat and shrimp.

The recipe calls for 1 cup uncooked rice, 1 cup chopped celery, 1/2 cup chopped green pepper, 3 green onions (finely sliced), 6 1/2 ounces sliced water chestnuts, 6 1/2 ounces of crab meat and 4 1/2 ounces of shrimp, 1 cup mayonnaise, 3/4 cup tomato juice, and grated Parmesan cheese.

Instead of cooking rice "as directed on the package label," use buckwheat (assuming that you have buckwheat and do not have any rice). Stir in celery, green peppers, green onions (if none available, substitute a couple of other vegetables that you like for the celery and green pepper and use a dash of onion powder in place of green onions), water chestnuts (try mushrooms or, perhaps, some finely chopped almonds), mayonnaise (or yogurt) and tomato juice.

In place of crab meat and shrimp, stir in finely diced steak meat and the can of tuna.

Transfer the mixture into a 2-quart baking dish and sprinkle with cheese. Bake in preheated oven for about 25 minutes. Then see if anyone can guess what it is that you've concocted.

There are any number of ways that will offer themselves to you while you are preparing meals at home to conserve, to substitute, and to backtrack. Use your imagination. If you follow this book's suggestions and tips on saving fuel while cooking, on making the most of the empty shelves at the supermarket or the grocery store, on growing your own vegetables, you will have already taken a giant step toward eliminating the ogre of shortages. But do not be satisfied with that. Keep your eyes and ears open, and your mind active with ideas. The momentum you should have built up by now will carry you effortlessly through otherwise frustrating situations.

Chapter 7

Water, Water—Is It Everywhere?

The United States Geological Survey hydrologists have estimated that of the 326 million cubic miles of water present on and under the surface of the Earth, man is able to utilize not more than one percent. Most of our water—the estimate is 317 million of the 326 million cubic miles, or more than 97%—is that briny, nausea-inducing broth of the oceans. Two of the remaining three percent, or some seven million cubic miles, is locked up in the ice caps of Antarctica and Greenland. Which leaves us some two million cubic miles of fresh water for irrigation, industrial purposes, and home use.

Two million cubic miles is quite a bit of water you might say. And it is. If it were stored in one storage tank, that tank would cover the entire continental United States and would be some 3700 feet high, assuming that it was constructed above the surface and that its bottom, or floor, was leveled out. But how long will this supply last us?

To begin with, there are now some *four billion* of us in the world. In 1971, USGS estimated that the daily per capita use of water in the United States—undoubtedly one of the world's largest users—was 1,600 gallons, in 1965. This was an average that was obtained from the total agricultural/industrial/domestic consumption. The USGS also estimated that the total water use in the United States would increase by 15% in 1970. Extrapolating that increase to 1975, we obtain a per capita consumption of water that equals 2,100 gallons—*per day!*

Let's use that figure as the hypothetical basis for the rest of the world. Multiplying four billion by 2,100, and then the product by 365, to obtain the total annual consumption of water, we get an almost incomprehensible figure of three quadrillion gallons! In cubic miles, that comes to 2,700.

That, you say, means that we have enough water to last us some 740 years. But we haven't accounted for population growth.

Twenty-five years from now, the increase in population (in 1969, the United Nations projection for the year 2000 sets a "medium" or most likely world population figure of 6.1 billion) will have set the No Water Date back from the year 2715 to the year 2470. By the year 2050, for which the United Nations projects a world population figure of *11 billion*, the No Water Date will have been rolled back to the year 2310.

There is a hypothesis (uncertain, to be sure) that by the year 2150, the world population will level off at 30 billion. The quantity of water that will have been consumed by then will equal *one million four hundred thousand cubic miles*—or almost 75% of the current supply of fresh water. How long will the remaining six hundred thousand cubic miles of water last for the 30 billion people in the year 2150?

For about 30 years.

So the population growth alone will have trimmed our fresh water supply by 535 years. Instead of having enough of it to last us until 2715, we will have enough until 2180. Give or take 50 years.

Of course, the above projection does not take into consideration a possible increase in the per capita consumption of water (similar to the 15% increase over the five-year period between 1965 and 1970 mentioned earlier), or the increase in pollution of water, which will be directly proportional to the increase in population growth. Neither does it take into consideration some positive factors, however. About 44% of the water consumed is "returnable" (it finds its way back into the original fresh-water supply), that desalting plants are already in operation around the world (the first large seawater-desalting plant having been built in Kuwait in 1949), and that you and I, and the four-billion-less-two others, do our bit in applying the Trident Principle to making the most of that cheapest of fluids without which, in some form, neither you nor I would be able to last more than eighteen hours.

Needless to say, few of us individually consume the daily "per capita" average of 2,100 gallons of water. Agriculture and industry make it seem as if we do. And there isn't very much we can do about *their* consumption of water, and they do consume a lot.

For example, to produce one gallon of gasoline, it is necessary to consume ten gallons of water. In producing one can of vegetables, the requirement is 10½ gallons of water. For producing one pound of paper, ten gallons are required. For one ton of woolen cloth, 160 gallons; for a ton of dry cement, 1,200 gallons; for a ton of steel, 5,200 gallons. Particularly, much water is required for the production of some relatively new types of articles: a ton of dacron requires *over one million gallons of water;* rayon, half a million; Kapron fiber, *one and a half million gallons!*

Obviously the most important step we, the consumers, can take is to awaken ourselves to the reality of the above figures and get involved in civil-action movements that will result in the construction of desalting plants wherever they are feasible and in the actualization of water-reclamation projects. And *then* we can do our little bit of conserving in our daily life.

Conserving Water in and Around the House

In domestic use, our water consumption is limited to the following areas: food preparation and direct internal consumption, washing and bathing, sanitation, gardening, sports (swimming pools), and entertainment (decorative fountains).

Consider the following hints and see if the suggestions offered don't painlessly cut down your water consumption to a considerable degree.

1. Water in the preparation of food. You can save water in the kitchen and in the bathroom without using any less of the fluid in your cooking than you need and without drinking any less water than you are accustomed to drinking. The conservation step is extremely simple, yet a great many of us don't take the trouble to make use of it. It involves the faucet; specifically, turning it off whenever the water coming out of it threatens to go directly down the drain.

The conservation here is unquestionably minimal, except in those cases where you do *not* fail to turn the faucet off as you rush toward the phone ringing in the living room to find that it's your long-lost friend calling who has so much to tell you that the glass of water you were going to drink turns into gallons of water gone into the city sewage system.

If you have a single faucet for both hot and cold water, give thought to converting it either to two separate faucets (which amounts to backtracking) or, if you are handy with plumbing tools or have a plumber/friend, to a triple-fauceted combination that will allow you immediately to turn on hot, cold, or warm water. The problem with the standard kitchen and bathroom fixture is that a lot of water is wasted before the right combination of hot and cold water is reached, unless a stopper is used in the basin, which doesn't do much good in the preparation of food. Consider as an alternative to the above a Dial-a-Temperature fixture, where the master control, which both adjusts the water flow and the hot-and-cold combination, allows you to turn on varying degrees of temperature—approximate but functional.

2. *Water in washing and bathing.* Unless you are just going to rinse out a few dishes or give your hands a quick wash, fill the sink or the washbasin with enough water to do the job, and use that water for the scrubbing phase. For rinsing, turn on the faucet and rinse quickly in the stream of fresh water. The same procedure applies to washing clothes.

If you have a washer-drier and/or dishwasher, use a full load in each. It takes no more water to wash a full load of dishes than it does to wash one or two items. Use proper detergents and settings, otherwise you may wind up having to repeat the wash, and that will require twice as much water as you would have needed had you done it right the first time.

If you like taking showers, see if you can get yourself in the habit of not turning the water on until you are already in the stall. Once in, either turn the water on slowly, adjusting the water temperature as you go, or turn on the cold water first—which will immediately fill you with unexpected vim and vigor and shudders—and then add hot water to the stream until you get the desired temperature.

Limit your singing to a repertoire that does not slide into Wagner's *Ring* cycle—and don't wave your hands in time with the music; keep washing yourself. Come out of the shower, having turned the water off, when you are clean, not when the song is finished. You can finish the song while you are toweling yourself dry!

If your preference is making like a fish in the bathtub, fill the bathtub to a point where the water level is two or three inches below the overflow opening—then get in. Better yet, get into the tub shortly after you've started the water going. At first you might feel as if you've just sat in a puddle, but that doesn't matter. You will be able to adjust the temperature as the water level is rising (which will eliminate the occasional necessity of having to let some water overflow or to pull the plug because the temperature of the bath water is too hot or too cold). You will also be better able to keep an *eye* on the water level and its proximity to the overflow drain.

If you like to rinse yourself in clean water, *don't* let all the water out and refill the tub; get under the shower instead. If your bathroom is not equipped with a shower, you can purchase a portable shower that consists merely of a hose with a shower head at one end and a connection for the faucet at the other. You will use but a fraction of the water to rinse yourself off this way as compared to refilling the bathtub.

Wash your hair while you are either taking a shower or a bath; you will use considerably less water in the long run.

For shaving, fill the washbasin with enough water to soak your face and then to rinse your razor. Don't keep the water running throughout your shave.

If you are not the shy kind, and if your tub is large enough, you may consider taking a bath with a friend. And remember, according to the *Daily Mirror*, "a true gentleman taking a bath *a deux* never, ever sinks the lady's plastic duck."

3. *Water in sanitation.* If you play poker, you should have no difficulty conserving water here. All you have to remember is that a royal flush always takes care of a full house. Install a larger tank if necessary—and don't waste ten gallons on a cigarette butt. Use an ashtray.

4. *Water in gardening.* If you are planting a garden, plant vegetation that does not require much water. Many herbs—thyme, parsley, rosemary, fennel, marjoram, and dill, for example—are decorative, useful, and require minimal watering. About an inch of water applied weekly to the soil surface will seep down to a depth of six inches, which is sufficient for herbaceous garden plants and grasses. Keep abreast of weather forecasts, letting the rain supply water for your plants whenever possible.

Flower gardens and rock gardens are other approaches to water-economizing landscaping that you may want to consider. Flowers require no more watering than do herbaceous plants. Rocks do not require any water at all. They just sit there—large boulders, small rocks, pebbles, gravel, and sand—looking permanently content and attractive when arranged with care.

Small trees and shrubs require considerably more water, so if there aren't any in your garden, consider yourself fortunate—unless, of course, you happen to have a stream traversing your property. If you do, the chances are that small, medium, and large trees and shrubs are already there, and the beautiful thing is that you will not have to worry about watering them. They get their water from the stream by way of underground seepage.

And, speaking of underground seepage, if you have a concealed, underground sprinkling system, make periodic checks of your lawn and garden for signs of water percolating up from damaged water conduits. This damage may be caused by any number of culprits, including gophers that chew their way through the water lines and shrub and tree roots that seek water, sense its presence, and then go for it.

5. *Water in swimming pools.* Many a swimming pool is nothing more than a status symbol. Few pool owners make anything more than token use of their water hole: They take an occasional quick dip, have a poolside barbecue or party, invite friends over for a swim. It is in a great many instances an investment that pays dividends only when the house where it has been installed goes on the market: It increases the value of the house—as well as property tax.

If you do have a pool, however, maintenance is unquestionably the most valuable water-conserving habit that you can get into. Keep the interior of the pool as clean as you possibly can; keep the surface of the water free of leaves and dirt; change the filter on the pump regularly and maintain that pump in top working order. When chlorinating the water, make absolutely certain of not "overdosing" it; neutralizers are, of course, available on the market, but it is best not to take any chances on having to empty and refill a twenty-thousand gallon hole in the ground with fresh water.

Make it one of *your* regulations—as it is in most of commercial and public pools—that anyone who goes swimming in your pool wears a cap. More havoc is caused in the filtering system by hair than by anything else.

If you do not have a pool, think twice before having one built. Go swimming at an ocean beach, in a lake or a river, or fill your bathtub with cold water, don your swimsuit, get in the tub and listen to your teeth chatter. Then go outside and take a suntan.

6. *Water in Fountains*. Unless you happen to have goldfish in the basin of your fountain, you can actually hook up your fountain to your water supply in such a way that not a drop is wasted. The system is relatively simple; the idea being to use the water for esthetically decorative purposes before using it for functional domestic consumption.

If it's an indoor fountain, you do not have to worry about water contamination. If it's an outdoor one, make certain its location is such that it can be maintained crystal-pure—away from cats, dogs, birds, and such. Have the main water line—or better yet, the water line that is leading to the bathtub cold-water faucet—lead to a water-storage tank with an automatic water inflow shutoff valve. This valve will be activated by the water level in the fountain basin, which, in turn, will be controlled by the cold-water faucet in the bathtub. A circulating water pump in the fountain will provide the aquatechnics.

PART THREE

Getting Around the Housing Pinch

If you want to move out of an apartment and become a home-owner, or if you want to buy a bigger house, this looks like about as good a time as the average buyer is likely to see. . . .

Thanks to the record-breaking pace of construction, the supply of houses on the market, both new and old, is very large. As a buyer, you are likely to have a fairly wide choice.

—U.S. News & World Report
(June 19, 1972)

If there is any symbol of the great American dream, it is "a home of your own." This is a goal of millions of families in impersonal apartments,

*second-story flats and dingy tenements. Recogniz-
ing this "possible dream," the federal government entered the housing field with a variety of
programs to encourage homeownership, especially
among middle- and lower-income families.*

—Family Circle (October 1972)

*. . . Villa Marina East, a Los Angeles real-estate
firm, put 231 half-built condominiums on sale at
prices ranging from $50,950 to a hefty $64,000.
Since the condos were crammed on 12½ acres with
an uninspiring view, potential buyers might have
been expected to ʰhumb their noses at the fancy
price tags. Not so. Within weeks, eager buyers
snatched up all the units and there's now a huge
waiting list for vacancies that grows longer every
day.*

—Newsweek (August 20, 1973)

*Cherished national myths have lately been crash-
ing down in alarming numbers. . . .*
*And, if that weren't enough, we seem due to
awaken from the greatest American dream of all
—that ours is a country where the avarage working man can realistically aspire to own his home.
. . .*
*Land, construction and financing costs have all
been rising sharply. According to Sen. John V.
Tunney (D-Calif.), 70% of adult wage earners
can't afford to own their own home.*

—John Pastier in Los Angeles Times
(May 13, 1974)

Chapter 8

If You Want to Rent or Lease

One of the greatest myths that we've succeeded in perpetrating upon ourselves is the conviction that there is a "housing pinch" in this country. Those of us in the nonhome-owning, middle-income bracket, scrambling as gracefully as we've been able to for that indefinable nonentity labeled "a better life," have been particularly susceptible to accepting the reality of that myth. The fact is: *There is no housing shortage.*

If you have had occasion to move recently from one rented dwelling to another, and if you consider yourself to be a member of the middle-income bracket, the chances are that you will vehemently disagree. "It took me three months," you will say, "to find this apartment (or this house)." As a matter of fact, I am a nonhome-owner in the middle-income bracket, and it took my wife and me close to *six* months to find the house we are currently living in. "He has put his foot in his mouth," you say? It took us six months to find a *house* that is *near schools* (elementary *and* secondary), is *large enough* for two adults and two children, has a large *yard/garden*, is owned by a landlord who doesn't mind his tenants having *two dogs, a cat, two rabbits, a guinea pig, a turtle*, is *isolated* enough so that the neighbors are not disturbed by the sounds that a practicing soprano accompanying herself on a piano emits, *and that is cheap*. It is also in a quiet neighborhood, yet within five minutes' drive of a bustling shopping center.

We found not so much (not at all, in fact) a shortage of dwellings as a shortage of dwellings that met our requirements. Some of those requirements are unquestionably important and justifiable, others are considerably less so. And specific requirements that are often extremely difficult to realize, especially when there is a parting of ways between the requirements that we want the sought-for dwelling to meet and the rental price we can afford to pay, are the obstacles that create the *impression* of a housing shortage.

Paradoxically, it seems, those in the lower-income bracket do not appear to be faced with the problem of finding suitable living quarters at an affordable price. Neither do those whose incomes range in the high-five-approaching-six-digit figures.

The reason is relatively clear and hinges on social attitudes and human nature. Those of us in the middle-income bracket are caught on the slippery slope between welfare and wealth and we will accept no alternative to edging upward. Our reasons may be any one or a combination of the following: conscious or sublimated fear of indigence or *signs* of it, fear of losing respect in the eyes of the swarm of those others inching their way up the slippery slope, dissatisfaction with the *status quo*, desire to improve our lot, ambition, concern for those whose lives to a greater or lesser degree will depend on our ability or inability to continue our climb, a desire or need to impress those above us.

In the same way, whenever we decide to move from one dwelling to another, we seek an improvement or improvements over our previous domicile, but we are forced to seek them at the lowest possible increase in cost.

The low-income person does not have these problems in most cases. In some instances he is content; in others, he is resigned to his financial limitations. In a great many cases he is patient, rational, and even happy and ulcer-free. He rents a room, an apartment, or a house that he can afford; he rents no more than he needs; he moves, but he moves not up the incline but horizontally at the bottom of the slope, often gathering his resources for a spectacular dash that now and then takes him right past us and to a firm ledge.

The high-income person seldom has any difficulty finding the right dwelling, and when he gets the urge to find one that is even "more right," he has few problems. Ready cash paves the way from one high plateau to the next.

Having hopefully thrown some light on the nature of the "housing pinch" and the pain of "the slippery slope," let's see how the pain of the pinch can be lessened or prevented in the search for a room, an apartment, and a house, with a rental or a lease in view.

And in the event you think we've finally come to a shortage that is outside the solution capabilities of the Trident Principle, think of *space*. You can *conserve* it, by using it; you can *substitute*, by turning what was designed to be a bedroom into a study, or den, or whatever; you can *backtrack*, by living in a communal dwelling, by hewing a log cabin, by living in a cave—and that *is* atavistic!

Finding a Home and Making the Most of It

Basically, the methods for finding any one type of dwelling (a room, for instance) are no different from those for another type (say, a house). It matters not whether you want a furnished room or an unfurnished house, you begin your search by either going through the classified ads of newspapers that service the area into which you wish to move, going to a real-estate agent whose territory you are planning to settle in, or setting out on a safari of For Rent/For Sale sign-hunting.

The first method is the least time-consuming, provided the phone numbers of the owner or agent are given, and may be used to judge the affordability of the area. Most metropolitan newspapers subdivide the area they are serving into sectors. A quick glance at the listings under each of these sectors will give you an idea as to which areas of the city or which suburbs offer rentals that fall within your budget.

The number of ads that will appear interesting to you will most likely exceed the number of places you will be able to inspect in one day. Call no more than you will be able to handle; make certain there will be someone there to show you around, and if necessary make an appointment. Consider the telephone number prefixes—identical prefixes are likely to be concentrated in locality, which will allow you to inspect more potential rentals. After you have obtained the addresses of, say, half a dozen places to go to, check these addresses on a map and plan your route so you will not have to retrace your steps.

The second method, employing a realtor or rental agency, should be disregarded if you are looking for a room to rent. It is not worth the realtor's time to handle rooms. If, however, you are apartment- or house-hunting, and if you do not mind paying a token fee (usually of about $10) in most cases, you may want to use an agent's services. To avoid frustration, state and get the facts. How much are you going to be charged and for what? Some fee agents charge a flat fee for a listing of addresses—and it is not unusual for these lists to be outdated. One of the houses listed on a list for which my wife and I had paid a $10 fee when we were house-hunting was a house that had been *sold three months earlier*. Another house did not exist: It had been torn down and an apartment complex was being constructed on the lot it had occupied, as well as on the lots adjacent to it.

So ascertain the reliability of the list; make sure the phone numbers, when included with the addresses, are correct. Many agents will not include the owners' telephone numbers; if you ask them, however, they will call—though perhaps grudgingly—two or three of the owners whose rental property is listed with their office. If on the other hand the agency refuses to check any listing for you, go to another agency.

Finally, there is the sign-hunting safari method. This approach is not recommended except in those cases where you've seen a large number of private rental signs within a limited area, or when you are looking for property to buy (although For Sale signs will in most cases lead you back to a realtor before you get a chance to inspect the property). In short, as the only or primary method of finding a dwelling for rent, the sign-hunt may prove to be extremely time-consuming and highly unrewarding. Use it as a secondary method, by keeping a lookout for such signs when you are driving to inspect a newspaper- or realtor-provided lead.

If you do happen to come across something of interest in the way of a potential rental, you will be unexpectedly rewarded; if you do not, you will not be disappointed.

The type of dwelling you rent should be determined by the function it will have in your life, the length of time you intend to spend in it (a week, a month, a year, or more), the number of people you expect it to house comfortably, and the monthly rental you are willing to pay.

1. *The function of the dwelling.* If you are a single individual and are not planning on doing any entertaining of guests, if you do not have any immediate plans of sharing your home life with anyone else, if, in other words, your life-style is such that the only function you expect of your residence is to provide you with a retreat in which you plan to do little other than rest (from work or from school) and sleep, a room or an efficiency apartment might be your best bet. The latter, usually consisting of a moderately large room with an adjoining kitchenette and bath, should be definitely considered above a room where bathroom facilities are often barely within walking distance and kitchen facilities are nonexistent. A room in a private home, if it is provided with a separate entrance and if it is not one of half a dozen cubicles occupied by mysterious strangers who are always in the bathroom when you have to use it, is another possibility you may look into.

Whatever you do, do not take the first room, apartment, or house, unless you *know* you are going to be satisfied there. At the same time, however, do not allow yourself to slip into becoming a victim of the "housing shortage" myth. Make a priority list of those elements that you would like the room, apartment, or house you are going to rent to have; then trim those priorities down to a list of *essentials.* The first of which should be its functionability, which includes location, size and number of rooms, proximity to your place of employment and/or schools, and degree of privacy the dwelling provides.

In addition to the three basic approaches to lining up a suitable dwelling (classified ads, realtors, and publicly displayed signs), do not dismiss the bulletin board as a medium to publicize your message. Most supermarkets have this free service, so if there is one or more such markets in the area that you would like to turn into your neighborhood, tack up one or more cards (4" x 5" will work fine) specifying what you are looking for on the market bulletin board. Be sure to include your phone number on the cards, as well as the time you can be reached at that number.

2. *Rental duration.* Very few of us, and those few very seldom, can ever be absolutely certain whether the dwelling we rent is going to house us for a month, six months, a year or longer. The uncertainties of modern life are so numerous and so great that it is often difficult for the average person to be confident even about such seeming predictables as what awaits him at work, at home, or in the mailbox. Nevertheless, we do have plans and expectations, and unless we are perennial nomads for one reason or another we do have a fairly firm idea of whether we are looking for a temporary lodging or a relatively permanent one.

This is generally an important consideration. It can be a critical one if you are offered a choice between renting an apartment or a house and leasing one. The rule of thumb to follow here is to rent if there is any uncertainty in your mind about the permanency of your job, about the regularity of your income, or about any other factor that many influence you into deciding to move again. A lease is a tie that binds, and breaking it can be expensive, especially if you sign a contract that empowers the lessor to collect all of the rent due through the termination of the lease if the lease is violated. On the other hand, if there is no uncertainty in your mind about your future, if your job is secure and your income guaranteed, a lease is an additional assurance of stability for you. It offers you the peace of mind of knowing that the property you are moving into will not put you in jeopardy through its being sold or demolished from under you. At least not without your being recompensed.

3. *How large a crowd are you?* If you are but a crowd of one, and unless you are in a line of business that requires extensive entertainment in the home, you should have no difficulty finding a rental unit suitable to your needs. You may even consider sharing an apartment with someone. If you are amenable to such an arrangement, the best place to find an apartment-to-share offer is any university campus bulletin board or tabloid paper. It would be advisable to spend at least a couple of hours with your prospective roommate before making the decision to move in. Such an arrangement does not only place a burden upon the apartment to be satisfactory to two relative strangers, but upon the two strangers (you and your roommate) to be compatible with each other.

Obviously, if there is a family involved in your life, you will want a dwelling sufficiently large to accommodate the three or the four of you, or however many of you there is. This means that you will want either an apartment or a house. Since most families have their own furniture, you will most likely wish to find a place that is unfurnished. Proceed in your hunt for a home in the manner described earlier, but while looking at each prospective rental unit, consider the possible ways in which you can do with less space than you think you need or ways in which you can do more with less.

If the children are young, and especially if they

are both (assuming there are two of them) boys, or both girls, a two-bedroom apartment or house could be more than adequate. Of course, it would be nice if each child had his or her own room. But is this *necessary?* As a matter of fact, even a one-bedroom home *might* be adequate, if there is a large living room and if you have a convertible couch or a sideboard table that converts into a bed. One-bedroom homes sometimes are more plentiful, and of course the rental is lower than that for a two-bedroom home in the same or comparable location.

4. *Consider your budget.* Whether you want to admit it or not, it will be your income that will determine the size, the location, and the type of dwelling you rent. The best way to make the most of this fact is not to fight it. If your monthly income before taxes is $600, your decision to rent a home for $300 per month would be a foolhardy one. Generally speaking, the percentage of income spent on rental should not exceed 30% of income that does not exceed $1000.00 per month before taxes. If you spend more than that, chances are you will find yourself tightening your budget belt to a point where financial cramps will ensue. Consider comfort and affordability above status symbolism or making impressions upon others. A small home can be just as elegant as a large one, and it is better to make a small dwelling work for you than to make a large one your heartless master.

There are further alternatives you may want to consider. If you live in the suburbs or the country, there are mobile homes and trailers and retired railroad cars. If there is a river or a lake close by, you may consider a houseboat. And if you live close to the ocean, a seaworthy fishing boat or sailboat can be a delightful substitute for the conventional dwelling. More on each of the above will be included in Chapter 11.

Chapter 9

If You Want to Buy

In 1968, the average purchase price of a new house in the United States was $19,400, its average size was 1,222 square feet, and the size of its lot was 9,178 square feet. By 1972, the average purchase price of a new home had risen by approximately 25%, to $24,250, its average size had increased by an almost unnoticeable four percent (or 51 square feet, the equivalent of a large walk-in closet) to 1,271 square feet, and the average size of the new lot had shrunk by 12% (or 1,130 square feet) to 8,048 square feet.

The selling price of used houses had in that period of time likewise taken a sharp increase. In Memphis, where the lowest increase was reported, a house that you could have bought for $25,800 in 1968, was priced at $28,800 four years later which was an almost 12% increase. In Miami, meanwhile, an area with the highest rise in used-house selling prices (close to 66%!), the house that would have cost you $21,000 in 1968 was priced at $34,800 four years later! And of course the mortgage interest rates have been climbing steadily over the past six years.

In short, as the editors of *Time* reported in their October 1, 1973, issue:

" . . . The land rush is powered in no small part by affluent people seeking second homes, [and] it is making the housing situation more crowded for the less fortunate. Lot prices now account for 24% of the total price of a typical new single-family home, up from 19% a decade ago. As lots become more expensive, developers try to keep profits up by constructing higher-priced houses or by building less house for the money—eliminating such features as patios and two-car garages. Soaring land values also lead many builders to put up "town houses" which are stuck together wall-to-wall. Other developments consist of misnamed 'mobile homes' (median price: $6,950), which are often trailers anchored to one spot. They are about all that buyers can afford after paying for the ground."

One of the reasons for the relatively grim picture that is being developed for the average working man or woman and his or her family is the fact that most of us are forced to settle down not so much where we want to, but where jobs, schools, hospitals, roads, and other features conducive to material comfort and convenience are located.

Essentially, then, the few facts presented above on housing costs add up to what obviously looks like a shortage of reasonably priced residential property. Home ownership is, indeed, rapidly becoming, as the staff of *Changing Times* put it in *Kiplinger's Family*

Buying Guide of fifteen years ago, "a symbol of prestige and achievement." In short, it is becoming *a status symbol* that progressively fewer people are able to afford. And there is a difference between buying something and being able to afford it!

So weigh with utmost seriousness your decision to buy a house. And remember that the number of years we think of as permanent is shrinking in inverse proportion to population growth: A hundred years ago you could buy a house in the country and sell it as a country home still twenty-five years later, while today a house in the country (within commuting distance of a city) is tomorrow's house in the suburbs and next week's victim of a freeway on-ramp or a shopping-center parking lot.

Of course, buying a home less for permanency than for profit is a different kettle of horses, or a fish of another color, *if* you are established in your career and can foresee steady employment and advancement. Otherwise, if the profit-making venture tempts you, remember that if circumstances forced you to unload the house before you've built up enough equity in it, or if the resale value of the house was less than the amount you paid for it—and neighborhoods do change for the worse as often as they change for the better—you would take a financial loss. The business of real estate, however, belongs no more in this book than do those horses in that fish kettle, so let's get to some particulars on home buying for residential purposes only.

One of the greatest problems that you will encounter in shopping for a house is finding the house you want *where* you want it and at a price you can *afford*. More than likely you may have to compromise somewhere along the line, although if such is the case you may be better off in the long run putting off buying your home until you *do* find precisely what you want and in the location you want it to be in.

If you have permanency in mind, look at each house with the eye of an interior (and exterior) decorator, especially if it's not a new house, and of an architect even if of an amateur one. An old but well-maintained house that appears smaller than what you had in mind, if situated on a large lot, may be expanded. A garage may be converted into another room or, if it's a large garage, into a couple of rooms. A bedroom may be added on to the existing house or, if the lot is sufficiently large for this, a guest house may be eventually put up in back of the house proper. (Such a guest house, incidentally, might be worth considering even if you would have no immediate personal use for it. Consider renting it. Its rental will pay you back for the cost of its construction within two to five years, depending on construction cost and rental price, and after that will bring in revenue to counter mortgage costs on the house proper.)

When looking at new houses, do not be swayed by the interior decoration, the furniture, the flowers on the dining room table, and the plastic fruit in a bowl on the kitchen sink counter. None of these are usually included in the price of the house that has been quoted to you. In many cases even the so-called built-in kitchen appliances (range, oven, dishwasher, refrigerator) are extra-cost options. So consider the house in its unfurnished state first; then consider it furnished with what you own. If you are thinking of buying new furniture, or possibly the furniture that is displayed in the house you look at, figure its cost at about 20% of the base price of the house. In other words, if the house you are looking at is selling for $25,000, you will probably have to pay another $5,000 (a low estimate) for the furniture it contains.

Whether it is a new house or a used one you are shopping for, never let it slip your mind that *you* are the one who is going to have to *live* in it and *pay* for it. Do not *ever* be *sold* a house; do not be compromised; listen to the real estate agent or the salesman with half an ear because the chances are that half of what he claims will never appear on the contract or will disappear when you move in. More than likely, if you are an average home buyer, you are going to work your butt off for the next twenty years or more to pay off the mortgage on the house, so *you* decide whether the house is "ideal," whether "it's the best buy you'll be able to find," whether its "advanced design" is worth the price you are going to have to pay for it.

And you *are* going to pay. As the previously mentioned *Time* feature story "The Land Boom" (October 1, 1973) puts it: "For most Americans, land-price inflation costs more than it is worth. For the homeowner, a rise in the value of his house is purely theoretical profit until he sells, but the land spiral meanwhile helps raise the price of almost everything that he must buy. Packing plants, bakeries, supermarkets, movie theaters, filling stations, widget makers—all pass on to their customers the rising prices —and taxes—that their owners must pay on the land on which they set up shop.

Do not fall into the trap of signing a contract on the basis of a "wishful guesstimate." In other words, if the price of a house is quoted to you at, say, $24,000, and the mortgage is for twenty years, do not divide $24,000 by twenty, which gives you $1,200, and then this last figure by twelve to get "the monthly expenditure" of $100. Such arithmetic is deadly! The interest on the mortgage, plus fire insurance and taxes, may very well double the figure of the above "guesstimate."

In addition, once you move into your own house you will promptly begin paying fuel and utility bills, bills for property taxes, trash collection, and maintenance. But prior to this will come the costs of taking over the house, of moving into it. The settlement costs may run to several hundred dollars, and the moving costs, such as hiring a van and paying for the telephone connection, may add up to another two hundred dollars.

So do not leap. Even consider a slight change in what you thought might be an ideal location. The further you move away from the city-central area, the lower is the price you will have to pay. There are some exceptions to this, of course, but generally speaking that is the rule. Thus, for example, the real estate price in the Miami Beach area can be as high as $450,000 per acre; property near Disney World runs from $900 per acre on the swampy southern fringe to $4,000 per acre on more stable ground north of Disney World; farm and grazing land in north-central Missouri can be bought for about $500 per acre.

Finally, consider the alternatives to the new or old *house*—specifically, condominium apartments, prefab homes, and trailers or mobile homes.

There are obvious immediate disadvantages in these three alternatives—the resale value of a condominium apartment will be more affected by the neighbors than a house will, and the prefab and mobile home depreciate in value—yet they are worth looking into as the first step toward owning your dream house. If you purchase a condominium apartment the monthly payments on which will be lower than what you are presently paying for rent, you may be not only saving but in the end realizing profit on the resale of the apartment. The same may be said of prefab and mobile homes if you *buy* rather than rent the lot on which you put either one of the two. And then you can start shopping for your dream home or even think of building it.

Chapter 10

If You Want to Build

Whether or not you are a professional architect or real estate developer, building your own home will probably be one of the high points in your life. If you can afford it—and in the long run building a home need not cost any more than buying a house—and/or if you have the time, it is a project suitable for anyone's list of goals. Not for any status reasons but for the reason of creative self-fulfillment. Undoubtedly those individuals for whom creativity is a commodity that may be purchased will not agree, primarily because they will not understand. However, anyone who has ever painted a picture, sewn a dress, planted a garden, built a television set, or overhauled a car's engine—almost anyone, in other words—will have an inkling of the pure pleasure of nonstatus-symbolic accomplishment the person who builds his own home will feel.

Building your own home is undoubtedly the best way to find a home perfectly suited to your needs. A great many of us do not consider this approach to solving the shortage of reasonably priced homes because there is a general feeling that it is "so much easier" to buy a house than it is to build one and because, erroneously, we believe that only the very rich can afford to build their own home.

Whether it is, in fact, "easier" to buy than it is to build is a controversial question. The ambiguity of the comparative adverb *easier* makes it controversial. It is unequivocally easier for you to lift a fifty-pound weight than it is to lift a hundred-pound weight, provided you do not alter your method of lifting it. If you utilize an assemblage of ropes and pulleys arranged to gain mechanical advantage, you have again made the term *easier* meaningless. The same holds true in regard to buying a home and building one. It all hinges on what is specifically meant by "easier," as well as what is meant by "build."

Undoubtedly it is easier for someone with an unlimited (relatively speaking) supply of money to *buy* a house that will very closely approximate the house he wants (assuming that he knows what he wants), than it is for someone with a limited bank account to *build* a house that meets all of the owner's requirements. Is it, however, "easier" to *buy* a $30,000 home for someone who has the sufficient down payment and a satisfactory credit rating for obtaining a mortgage, than it is, for the same person, to build that $30,000 home?

If you look at it in terms of *labor*, it is true that in buying a home you will not be involved in the physical labor of surveying the land, leveling the ground, laying the foundation, erecting the exterior walls, raising the roof, laying the floors, finishing the interior and the exterior, installing door and window frames, and finally landscaping the grounds.

However, regular maintenance and repair of a purchased home will keep you busy with the hammer, the screwdriver, the assorted wrenches, the saw, and the paint brush almost from the day you move in. Furthermore, unless you buy a house shortly before you retire or immediately upon retirement (and do not be too optimistic about becoming a homeowner if you are in your sixties unless you have enough money stashed away in the bank and/or a pension that is adequate), you *will* labor for the fifteen, twenty, twenty-five, or thirty years that it will take you to pay the mortgage off. You will labor at the office or the store or the factory, and you will labor for considerably longer than necesary; in fact, you will most likely be laboring to make the mortgage payments long after the *house* has been paid off! Like for eighteen years after!

If you find that difficult to believe, let's take a specific example. A full-page ad in the June 9, 1974, issue of *Los Angeles Times*, placed by The Larwin Group, Inc., urges you to buy one of their homes, to "take advantage" of their 8 1/4% financing rate. Let's suppose you were going to buy one of their $30,000 homes. Let's say you put down 20% on the house, or $6,000. That left you a "balance" of $24,000, right? (Hint: there's a reason for those quotation marks around that word *balance*). To answer the question, let's quote directly from the ad:

... TYPICAL FINANCING: For a $30,000 home (cash price), 20% down payment of $6,000. First trust deed of $24,000 paid in 354 equal monthly payments of $181.31 principal and interest at 8 1/4% simple annual rate, 8.9% ANNUAL

PERCENTAGE RATE. No Second Trust Deed.

What does this mean? It means that you will be paying off the "balance" of $24,000 for 29½ years and by the time you will have made your last (354th) payment you will have paid off $64,183.74! On top of the $6,000 down payment. Your $30,000 home, in other words, by the time you own it, will have cost you over $70,000! On the balance owing, you will have paid $24,000 in principal—and $40,183.74 *in interest!*

A home with a $40,000 price tag will have cost you a sum of $53,462.68 in interest alone. Add to that the 20% down payment of $8,000 and the $32,000 "balance" or principal, and the final total of your payments on it will add up to $93,462.68!

Now, that argument about "only the rich being able to build their own home" becomes somewhat suspect. It is obvious from the above figures that if you can afford to buy a home that sells for $30,000, you can afford to build a $60,000 home. It's as simple as that. And the choice is yours as to whether you want to live in a $30,000 mass-produced house-development unit for which you had paid $60,000 or whether you want to live in a personally designed $60,000 dwelling that had cost $60,000 to build. Or $45,000. Or $30,000.

How do you go about building your own home? Where do you start? And how long will it take you to have it ready for a housewarming party?

To begin with, decide on what kind of house you want. It may be a house you've lived in; it may be a house you've passed on the road somewhere; it may be a house you've seen in one of the homemakers' or homeowners' magazines. Or it may be a house that exists only in your mind, a house you've been dreaming of owning, perhaps even of building. In short, it may be a house for which blueprints are already available or it may be a house that starts with a sketch, a rough floor plan drawn on a paper napkin. It may be conventional—a ranch house, a tract home, a two-storied American modern—or it may be an unconventional one—a circular dwelling on swiveling pylons that shut off the multientranced parking area underneath the streamlined-donut shape of the living quarters, with a fountain in the center of the carport area shooting plumes of water above the level of the interior balcony that overlooks the waterworks and surrounds it.

Next, decide on the location, not necessarily a specific one at this point. Do you want your house to rise within the city limits, in the suburbs, in the foothills or the mountains, in a valley, on the bank of a river, a lake, or a stream or perhaps on the ocean or overlooking it, or in the desert? Compromise on the location if you have to. Remember that the grass may be greener in more than one place. Then start shopping around for land.

To compensate for the expenditures that will arise once you start your home-building project, consider either moving into a cheaper apartment or house than the one you've been paying rental on or putting up temporary quarters on your land once that is purchased. It is assumed that you will pay cash for the property, an amount which should not exceed the amount that would be required for a down payment on any house you may have considered buying.

Incidentally, beware of the numerous land swindles that are being perpetrated upon the unwary readers of some periodicals in which land is sold by way of ads for incredibly low prices because, unknown to you until you visit your mail-order acquired lot, the land is in the majority of cases incredibly useless. A friend of mine bought "a half-acre of breathtaking tropical paradise" sight unseen for $500. It took him a while to find it when he finally got around to looking at his purchase. It was under three feet of water, the closest dry land was 50 feet away, and it was part of a wildlife refuge—owned by the government.

Having bought your property, then, proceed by superimposing the plan of your house over the map of the land for optimum utilization of daylight and utilities and sanitation hookup, assuming that the site you selected has public provisions of the latter. If it does not, you may have to consider alternatives: utilizing the running water of the stream for generating electric power, or, in the absence of a stream, incorporating solar energy panels into the design of your home; butane or natural gas is another alternative; water may be tapped from the stream, drawn from a well, or stored in a water tank; a cistern or cesspool might have to be installed to take care of the sewage and sanitation problem. Hopefully, of course, you will have considered all of the above *before* buying the land.

Construction plans for your home, consisting of detailed blueprints, will be an expensive item, particularly if it is an original design that requires an architect's knowledge. You can save a considerable amount of money here, however, by either conscripting the services of an advanced architectural student or of a recent architectural school graduate. Regardless of who it is that prepares the plans for the construction of your home, be absolutely certain that none of the features violate the local building codes and regulations. If you hire a professional architect, whose standard fee is about 15% of the total cost of construction, he will take over the entire operation. An alternative is to have an architect prepare some rough plans which you, in turn, take to a builder for detailing.

The actual construction of your home can be undertaken in any number of ways, the selection of which should primarily depend on five factors: your financial resources, your free time, your courage, your dexterity with tools, and your ability to read construction plans or blueprints.

If you are financially prepared to delegate the entire construction of your house to the architect, the builder-contractor, the carpenter, the electrician, and the plumber, your $30,000 home will actually cost you in the neighborhood of $30,000. You can cut on the final cost here by utilizing indigenous building materials for the construction of your house if such materials are available.

There is the case, for example, of an architect who bought five acres of government surplus land in southwestern South Dakota. The ground was all but invisible. Rocks of every size imaginable, some approaching boulder dimensions, made up the landscape. The architect rearranged the debris into the shape of a four-bedroom house. All it took was ingenuity, a bulldozer, and $5,000 worth of nonindigenous materials: some lumber, roofing material, and glass. The appraisal value of the house was placed at $45,000. The cost? The only answer the architect is willing to give is a sly smile.

Your free time, as well as the free time of your friends and relatives, is a deciding factor on how much of the actual work you can do yourself. Building a house is a lot of work, even with all of the labor-saving tools you may be able to rent or borrow. To get an idea of how long it will take you to build your home, get a man-hours labor estimate from a builder-contractor, then add about ten percent more to the time he quotes you to make up for the fact that, being a new experience for you, it will take understandably longer. Of course, if there will be three or four of you working on the house, divide the man-hour figure by three or four. For example, if you are given the estimate of 2,000 man-hours, it means that it would take 20 men 12½ eight-hour days to complete the project. For you alone, working four hours each day and sixteen hours over the weekends, it would take 14 months, plus a month and a half—the "inexperience factor."

Your dexterity with tools and your ability to read construction plans will definitely be an advantage; your courage to tackle the job in spite of the fact that your tool-handling is amateurish and your blueprint-reading requires practice may in the long run be the difference between your home being finished by you and your home being finished by a building construction team. Do not, however, let your courage get in the way of your reason. If the project becomes too much, seek professional help. There hasn't been a single brave man who hasn't faltered.

Chapter 11

Alternatives to the Standard Residence

If you feel that neither building nor buying a home is for you, if you are tired of supporting your apartment or house landlord, if you do not mind breaking the old homesteader's tradition that demands a home that sits solidly upon the ground, that possesses a permanent address, and that symbolizes your social conformity, you may find that some of the alternatives to the standard home are as good an answer as any to the housing shortage.

Actually two of these alternatives, or *substitutions,* are being widely utilized throughout the country, although perhaps more as second homes than as replacements for the conventional home. These two are house trailers and mobile homes. You see them on the road, you see them at campgrounds; they raise their TV aerials from behind fences in the city as well as in the country.

You can rent them, you can buy them, and if you are not burdened by a houseful of furniture, these as well as the other alternatives to the standard, concrete-foundation-based home may strike your fancy and solve your house-hunting problems as well. And of course one of the beauties of these "homes on wheels or blocks" is their mobility. If you change jobs, you can take your home with you, whether it be to the other end of town or to another state. In the case of a trailer, it can be your vacation home, since all you have to do is take it wherever you are going on your vacation and park it. For all practical purposes, it eliminates your motel and hotel bills.

A mobile home is often of a size that makes the idea of taking it on vacation with you ludicrous. But it *is* transportable whenever you are faced with making a major move. Furthermore, there is no reason, other than the fuel crisis, why you could not own a mobile home *and* a house trailer. The combination of the two would offer you the kind of freedom and flexibility that might be just the prescription you need for getting out of the proverbial rut of big-city living.

Both mobile homes and house trailers come in an assortment of sizes and prices. You may purchase either one in a "stripped" form—that is, minus any furnishings, at much less than the price of a fully equipped model.

One of the disadvantages of mobile homes is their rapid depreciation, particularly in the first year. You may, for example, have difficulty getting more than $7,500 for a mobile home a year after you had paid $10,000 for it. If you are, however, more interested in getting *use* out of it than a monetary return on your investment, with regular maintenance and repair you will get as much money out of a mobile home as you will out of any other, standard, dwelling.

If you feel that you are going to remain within one area for a relatively long time, consider buying a *lot* to anchor your mobile home in rather than renting a space. As Ernest Callenbach points out in his book *Living Poor With Style:*

> . . . the greatest practical disadvantage of trailer living at present is that unless you own or can lease land in the country . . . you will have to keep your trailer in a trailer park. These are generally disliked by the middle-class citizenry, and confined by zoning rules to the neighborhood of junkyards or tawdry highway strip developments. Then the operators jam the spaces together so that you are sometimes lucky to get your door open without scraping the trailer next to you. Tree or shade is nonexistent, but concrete is abundant. . . .

You may, and rightly, disagree with Callenbach, since there are trailer and mobile-home parks that belie everything he says. Note, however, the title of his book and accept his word on trailer parks if you are not willing to pay exorbitant rental for a chunk of ground to berth your 25-, 30-, or 35-and-up-footer in.

Undoubtedly one of the reasons some seven million or more Americans are now living in mobile homes is the price. You can buy a mobile home for anywhere from $4,500—for the smallest one-bedroom model— to $18,000—for a relatively large three-bedroom, two-bath model with central air conditioning—and more— for a thoroughly lavish model. You can usually acquire a mobile home for a cash down payment of somewhere between $1,000 and $2,000. And the monthly cost for an average home, including monthly costs in a park as well as the monthly installment payments, can run around $175 to $200.

Although buying a lot for the trailer—the price for which could range from $2,000 to $5,000—does present the additional expense of providing utilities, such as water, gas, electricity, and sewage system, the price of land going up as it is doing, you may wind up with a profit when you decide to sell the property.

Communal Living

While we are still on dry land, that is, before we go on to consider houseboats and sailing or motor vessels, a word or two should be said about communal living.

This approach to both beating the housing shortage and the skyrocketing cost of living has been thoroughly written up, both pro and con, in innumerable articles and a great number of books that have hit the stands within the past decade. The concept is of course not a new one. It was practiced by our long-gone predecessors in the time before the dragons and is still practiced with relative success by some of the primitive tribes that have managed to keep out of the helter-skelter dash of civilization.

It should be pointed out that the primitive tribes appear to have more on the ball as far as this lifestyle goes than we do. Specifically, not many of the communes that have been started in the United States have had a longevity that would encourage one to embark on such an adventure. Perhaps the main reason for the high percentage of failures of communal living attempts is the fact that human beings are not yet advanced enough on the evolutionary scale—or possibly too "advanced," i.e., spoiled by societal mores and scientific technology—to be ready for "an ideal society," which is what communes set out to be.

An ideal society cannot be formed except by and of

133

ideal members. And no member is ever ideal enough except to himself. The rate of divorces in the United States is an indirect proof of this. If *two* people find it difficult to coexist in harmony, how can five, ten, or fifteen do so?

Unquestionably, there are material advantages to an arrangement where a group—say, of ten people— shares the expenses of a single home. If such a group is made up of three families, and if there is a bread-winner in each of these families, then the rental expenses, for example, being shared, are greatly reduced. This kind of thinking, however, of itself destroys the concept of communal living since it breaks up the unity that the group is intended to have. The complexity of a commune is such that unless all of the members are perfectly attuned to their rights and responsibilities, unless each and every member of the commune is able to think in terms of "us" meaning the commune, rather than in terms of "us" meaning his immediate family—or worse yet of "me" the individual—the commune becomes unworkable.

There are those undoubtedly who will bring up the success of the *kibbutzim* in Israel as an example of workable communal living. Members of *kibbutzim* generally share a common ideology such as Jewish orthodoxy, ethical humanism, and social utopianism. They typically work without pay and are supplied with individual housing, medical care, clothing, as well as other personal needs. They have central kitchens and dining rooms, communal kindergartens, and often children's dormitories where the children live apart from their parents. And these communes have been successful since the turn of the century.

True. The question arises, however, whether their success should not be attributed primarily to the same *external* type of situation that has made the Tasaday tribe of Mindanao a communal success: namely, the external threat of war in the first case and of the jungle in the second. Even the firm beliefs of both the Jews of Israel and the Tasaday of the Philippines, something that is extremely vacuous in our country, might have contributed to their success at a form of utopianism. There is a parallel between the still expected Messiah of the Jews and the belief of the Tasaday: "Our ancestors told us never to leave this place of ours. They told us the god of our people would come if we remained here."

Yet the fact that one of the most advanced societies and one of the most primitive ones do appear to make communal living work, does point to the potential of communal living. It does, however, require a selflessness and a serious approach that few of us have been able to bring to our ventures into utopianism.

Home on Water

The two remaining alternatives to conventional homes have to do with living on water. The idea might be far away from anything you may have ever contemplated. Do give it a thought, however, if there happens to be a navigable river or a lake, or an ocean within commuting distance of your job. If there isn't, perhaps you have been thinking of buying a waterfront home upon retirement.

The final two alternatives do not include a waterfront lot; they do, however, include the unlimited expanse of the waters.

If rivers and lakes are your weakness, consider the houseboat. If the sea brings a spark to your eye, ponder over the possibility of owning a sailing vessel that is not quite a yacht but is large enough to be a permanent home. And do not brush the idea aside because you feel you can't afford a boat. Maybe you can.

A houseboat is essentially a mobile home that floats,

and the price of a houseboat is as a rule comparable to the price of a mobile home of the same size. Furthermore, you can buy an unfurnished houseboat almost as easily as you can an unfurnished house, mobile home or condominium apartment. All you need to know is where to look, which includes the classified ads of a resort or port-city newspaper and specialized publications such as *Boating, Canadian Sailing, Go Boating, Lakeland Boating, Motor Boating and Sailing, Rudder,* and *Sail,* to name the major ones.

If you are one of those people who just can't lay the hammer down, there is no reason why you cannot build either a houseboat or a sailboat yourself. There are plans and patterns available from a number of marine designers at nominal cost.

Glen L. Marine Designs, for example, offer plans for a 33-foot houseboat that provides all the comforts of a modern apartment with private sleeping quarters for three couples, their Delta King. The price of plans and patterns is $49.00. Clark Craft, of Tonawanda, New York, likewise offer several designs of houseboat. Their paper patterns and large scale plans for a comparable 33-foot houseboat sell for $6,000. These consist of large-scale blueprints especially intended for the amateur builder (the construction, incidentally, is of plywood) as well as an instruction booklet that describes the building of the boat in step-by-step detail. In addition to that you get a complete bill of materials that you will need to see your boat to the final stages of construction.

Unless you have had thorough training in naval engineering and architecture, it is best not to attempt designing your own boat, especially of the seagoing variety. Trust the masters. Besides, there are innumerable designs to pick from. Visit boat shows whenever they are presented; most major sea ports have one or two a year on a regular basis. Look the boats over, go through them, study their interior layout, note the construction materials used, observe the type of rigging they are provided with, and check to see if they are equipped with an auxiliary motor. Take all the literature you are able to obtain; then, having decided on the type of boat that you feel will make the best home, buy it—or build it.

What will probably sell you on a certain boat will be the boat's interior layout. In most cases it can be reproduced, or very closely approximated, on any other boat of equal dimensions. The primary decision you will have to make, following the decision to build the boat, is the type of material you will want to use for constructing the hull of the boat.

The three choices you have are fiberglass, wood, or ferro-cement. If you decide on fiberglass, you will not have to build the hull. You will not be *able* to build the hull, since fiberglass hulls are molded. So if it's a fiberglass boat you've decided on, you buy the hull and proceed with finishing the interior and building the superstructure. What you save on labor is considerable.

A 32-foot fiberglass hull will cost you in the vicinity of $6,000. A 42-foot ferro-cement hull, deck, and superstructure may cost you half that amount, if you build it yourself. There is not much difference in cost or labor between building a wooden hull and a ferro-cement one. If you've never built a boat before, however, the ferro-cement construction may be your wisest choice. The work may be more tedious—a 42-foot hull will require your tying 45,000 chicken-wire ties to form a mesh on which the cement is applied—but there is considerably less chance of inadvertent miscalculation if you follow instructions. And the final product, your boat, is reputed to be all but unsinkable —unless it is possibly torpedoed—if made of ferro-cement.

The final cost on any of the above will approximately equal that of a medium-priced home, only your home—providing you conscientiously complete a course in seamanship—will have the capability of taking you around the world. And that's a tempting trip to consider when, or even before, retirement time comes around.

PART FOUR

THE COMET'S TAIL—
A MISCELLANY OF SHORTAGES

There is enough in the world for everyone to have plenty to live on happily and to be at peace with his neighbors.

— Harry S. Truman, *Memoirs* (1955)

On top of the rising costs of food, gasoline and rent, inflation-riddled Americans now have still another worry. . . . Prices of clothes and most other textile goods are climbing . . . for a wide variety of reasons: threadbare supplies, bad weather, questionable Government policies and heavy foreign demand. In addition to the shortage of natural fibers, a scarcity of synthetics looms. . . .

Silk is in short supply. . . . Wool is scarce. . . .
Cotton is the most widely used natural fiber, but
. . . is no longer very stable. Demand for all grades
is . . . greatly outstripping supply. . . .

—*Time* (December 3, 1973)

. . . Many industries could not keep pace with de-
mand because plants making such basic materials as
steel, cement and paper were strained to capacity. . . .
The problem was compounded by scarcities of such
raw materials as wheat, lumber and cotton. . . .

—*Time* (January 14, 1974)

Lack of money is the root of all evil.

—George Bernard Shaw,
Man and Superman

Chapter 12

Furnishings: Home and Personal

If you have had the occasion to walk through a furniture or a clothing store recently, as undoubtedly you have, one impression you were probably *not* left with was that there was a noticeable shortage of anything. Armchairs, sofas, beds, dressing tables, bookcases, drapes, carpets, throw rugs, dresses, shirts, slacks, shoes, suits, or anything else you could think of installing in your home or putting on yourself was there—in every shape, design, color, and size imaginable. And if you purchased what you wanted without giving the price you paid a second thought, then you are one of the fortunate few untouched by inflation.

If, however, you purchased nothing, if you drove any appreciable distance to and from the shopping center and spent several hours just window-shopping, or if you made a minor purchase reluctantly, then you are probably a victim of what might be called "a shortage within the horn of plenty." The effect of an abundance of prohibitively priced items is no different from a shortage, or even nonexistence, of such items. A shortage of home furnishings or clothing, however, whether that shortage is real by reason of nonbeing or of pricing, is considerably less critical than a food or water shortage and can be quite easily counteracted by you if you again lean on the Trident Principle.

Your Home Furnishings and the Trident Principle

Conserving what you have in the way of furniture and accessories is probably the most effective way to become oblivious to the price tags in furniture stores. It involves nothing more than treating your furniture, your rugs, and your drapes as if you were going to have them forever. Convince yourself that your dining-room table, for example, is an antique, worth ten times more than what it actually is. You may find yourself polishing it more often, tightening whatever loose screws it might have, or even refinishing it.

Look at that couch of yours, the one you were thinking of replacing with a new one. Does it really *need* replacing? Won't shampooing it restore it to close to its original appearance? If it needs reupholstering, even if its springs tend to get fresh with you every time you sit down, it is not beyond restoring. And to have that done at minimal cost, do it yourself. Re-upholstering a couch is a fascinating and challenging project. It's been compared to putting a pair of pajamas on a kangaroo or stuffing a dinosaur!

Dust, wax, or polish all of your furniture woodwork periodically. If there are children in the family, impress upon them that beds and couches are not trampolines, that the seat of the chair is designed for a specific part of the human anatomy and that feet aren't it. If there is a cigarette smoker in the house, institute a law that butts are to be found only where they belong, specifically, in the ashtray and attended to by the smoker at all times, not left teetering precariously between the inside of the ashtray and the surface of the table. Leaving burning cigarettes unattended is not only hazardous to your furniture but to your entire house and the people in it as well.

The Japanese have had a custom, which is slowly being erased by Western influence, that might very well be worthwhile picking up. It involves nothing more than removing footgear before entering a residence. Such a habit eliminates outside dust and dirt from being dragged in on the soles of the shoes, which cuts down on your carpet-vacuuming frequency, which in turn decreases the wear and tear on the rug. Furthermore, by leaving your shoes outside—or by taking them off outside and then depositing them in entry hallway closet—you leave the scuff marks totally inert on your shoes rather than on the hardwood floors. The only problem with the honorable Japanese custom is that if you have children, who find enormous enjoyment in transporting themselves in and out of the house in a constantly repeating cycle, the ritual does not seem to work. Somewhere between the inside and the outside of the house, the children, especially those below college age, have a tendency to become confused: Their shoes wind up somewhere in the house (don't be surprised to find them in the refrigerator, for example!) while their bare or stockinged feet, along with the rest of them, wind up outside. The end result is that all sorts of things that shoes would not normally carry into the house are carried in by way of socks and/or bare feet.

Pets, particularly long-haired dogs, are even worse offenders in this respect. If your dog has free access in and out of the house, and if you have a garden or a yard that has, perhaps, a bit more vegetation in it than it ideally should—vegetation of the foxtail grass variety, for example—your dog will appear to be working on the project of bringing as much of the garden into the house as it possibly can, both in its mouth and its hair. And foxtails have their bizarre streak of stubborness in them once they wind up on your carpet. Few vacuum cleaners are powerful enough to dislodge them; they anchor themselves within the rug pile and refuse to budge. The only way you can evict these bristles of dry grass is by dislodging each one manually. Foxtails, incidentally, can be dangerous to pets, if they lodge in ears or eyes.

Conserving, that is, taking proper care, of the furniture and other house accessories that you have is not at all difficult once you reject the philosophy that "replacement of the old by the new" is essential to the enjoyment of life. If you have a cocktail table or coffee table that has nothing going against it other than its age, and if that age does not show, there is no reason in the world why you should feel obliged to replace it, especially if doing so would force you to tighten your budget. The same holds true for any other serviceable items of furniture, carpetry, or drapery in your home.

Remember that every antique you see is nothing more than an old item well preserved.

Substitution, the second approach to making the Trident Principle work for you in your home furnishings dilemma, overlaps the production end of the conservation stage (building your own, and substituting such home-made pieces of furniture and accessories for those that are no longer serviceable, instead of buying) as well as the backtracking stage (building your own *is* backtracking).

There are a number of furniture items that most of us should *not* attempt to construct in our workshop or garage. Among these are large upholstered pieces of furniture, such as sofas, armchairs, bed mattresses. The combination of springwork, padding, upholstering, and woodwork is as a rule too much to tackle if you are a novice in the furniture-making trade. Aside from these, however, with a bit of patience, you should have no difficulty in creating a pair of side tables of your own design, if you have a leaning in that direction, or recreating practically any item of furniture that you may find in the most expensive furniture store, at a cost that is seldom more than a fourth of the selling price, and usually is much lower than that.

Start with relatively simple projects, projects that will not be marred by slight imperfections of amateur workmanship. A rustic picnic table and benches set for the patio is an excellent project for your carpenter's debut. You probably already have all the tools you'll need around the house—a power saw, a set of screwdrivers and/or a hammer. You may even manage without a saw; most home-improvement centers and lumberyards where you would go to purchase the lumber for a project such as this one will cut the wood you buy to specifications for a nominal fee.

Avoid working with curved surfaces in the beginning; it is much more difficult to build a round-topped table than a square- or rectangular-topped one. Eventually, you will become skilled enough to create a cocktail table with an intricate French curve design; until, however, you get to feel fairly comfortable working with wood and carpentry tools, work on projects that are not complex enough to discourage you, progressing gradually from the picnic table set to an end table to a night stand, a chair, and so forth, leaving the intricate sideboard and buffet for later.

There are shelves and shelves of books on do-it-yourself projects at your local library. Pick up a few, read them, buy some lumber—most handbooks specify exactly what kind of wood and how much of it you will need for each project—and go to it. You may feel by the time you get through building that *guéridon* table that you had missed your calling.

As long as you are backtracking, consider making use of orange crates and whatever odd pieces of lumber you may have been moving from one end of your attic or garage to another. Use your imagination, use your ingenuity, and use the Trident Principle.

Your Clothing and the Trident Principle

Much that was said about home furnishings applies to the clothing you wear. While it is impossible to make clothing—particularly children's clothing—that lasts as long as a dining-room set, with proper care, clothing *can* be made to last considerably longer than it normally does.

Caring while wearing, and wearing only those clothes that are suitable for the occasion—old jeans, for example, when working in your garden or going on a fishing trip—will add life to your wardrobe. Learning to hang the dresses, shirts, slacks, and sweaters on hangers immediately upon taking them off—and particularly getting the children into this habit—will further cut down on your need to buy a new set of clothing every other month or every month, whatever the case might be. You may have a problem getting Junior to do this—he will undoubtedly insist that changing in and out of his playclothes is "wearing him and his clothing out"—but persist; eventually, he will get tired of your nagging.

Regular maintenance of clothing requires very little effort. Buttons, one sometimes gets the impression, were designed to come off shirt cuffs and shirt fronts and sweaters. Sewing on a button, however, is as simple as pricking a finger, and after a while gets to be a lot less painful. Besides, a button costs considerably less than a new shirt or jacket. A missing button is not sufficient reason to relegate the buttonless item to play- or work-clothes status.

Sewing your own clothes, knitting, crocheting, are other skills you might want to learn. Consider "recycling" some of your clothes or accessories. *Woman's Day* (August, 1972), for example, suggests converting your scarves into smocks, blouses, bags, and skirts, as well as exclusively designed hats. Making your own clothes even out of new textile materials will not only guarantee you a savings but, in quite a number of instances, an opportunity to create your own style or recreate a Saks Fifth Avenue or Magnin's "original."

Chapter 13

The Question of Professional Services

Few of us go through life without ever requiring the services of an attorney, dentist, physician, psychiatrist, or some other specialist. Depending on whether you live in the city, suburb, or country—and depending upon your financial resources—you may or may not find difficulty in obtaining the services you need.

In fact, with the ratio of professionals (in any specific category) to nonprofessionals being what it is—one attorney, for example, for every 65 people, one dentist for every 277 potential dental clients (or 8864 teeth), one physician for every 124 persons (the figures are conservative—based on new people entering the professions in 1970-71)—even strong financial resources often do not speak as loudly as you would expect them to. And if your bank account isn't geared for handling emergency situations at all, the end result can be catastrophic in more ways than one.

So how do you handle the problem of finding an attorney who will defend your interests in court, a doctor who will examine your throat the moment you say "ah," a surgeon who will remove your appendix in time and not take your billfold with it, a psychiatrist who will ease your emotional upheaval or mental fatigue without turning you into a permanent cover for his couch, or a veterinarian who will try to do as much for your mongrel as he will for a pedigreed show-dog champion? Waiting for your children to grow up and bail you out of this kind of shortage by becoming professional specialists is not very practical.

Obviously the only long-term solution to the problem is encouraging young people to go into those professions that show signs of manpower shortage and at the same time keeping a lid on population growth. But this solution is not of much immediate use to you. What you are left with is the Trident Principle.

Conservation Is the First Approach

Trying to maintain the *status quo*—legally, physically, mentally, and emotionally, as well as financially —should theoretically keep your need for such professional services to a minimum. The only threat such an approach would hold, providing everyone conspired to follow it, would be to the livelihood of attorneys, physicians, dentists, and other professionals of similar ilk. Such conservation procedure, as a matter of fact, is being indirectly implemented in New Zealand by that country's government-sponsored and all-inclusive accident insurance program.

It provides that anyone, whether a resident of

New Zealand or a tourist, who meets with any kind of accident while within the territorial limits of that country is automatically recompensed by the government from a special accident-insurance fund set up for that purpose and maintained by a fraction of New Zealand's income-tax revenue. This approach eliminates litigations of cases spurred by accidents and thereby frees the attorneys to pursue their practice in other areas of the law. It is also said to act as a damper on people's carelessness, since it makes totally impossible the collection of some astronomical sum from the owners of a building, for example, in front of which a careless pedestrian might have broken his leg. The accident victim cannot sue the owner of the building for negligence. And, of course, a decline in the accident rate increases the time available to the country's physicians, surgeons, and dentists to treat those patients whose ailments are brought about by factors other than carelessness.

Similarly, if you exercise caution in your everyday dealings, both public and private, if you avoid legally questionable transactions, and if you are habitually alert to protect your interests, there may never be any need for you to seek legal advice. If you maintain a proper diet, engage regularly in exercise for the health of it, get the proper rest your body requires, and take yourself for regular physical checkups, the chances are that you will live to a happy and ripe old age. Finally, if you let reason guide your actions and principles—and if you're lucky—you may never have to see the interior of a psychiatrist's office.

Substitution Within Reason

Obviously, substitution does not mean that you should get your lawyer to extract your teeth or go to the vet with your emotional problems. It does, however, mean that in noncritical cases—and if you follow the conservation approach faithfully you should have very few critical cases—you should be reasonable in your selection of professionals. If you carry medical insurance (and you definitely should), and if that medical insurance is tied in with a specific clinic, do not wait to see the Dr. X who had treated you previously at that clinic if he is not available, or if to see him you have to place your name on a three-week waiting list. Settle for Dr. Y or Dr. Z. Either one will be able to tell from your medical file, with no more difficulty than Dr. X would, what your specific problem might be, what you are allergic to, and what method of treatment is indicated.

Remember that with the number of patients who go through a doctor's office, rare and unwise is the physician who will remember you well enough to treat you without checking and studying your medical record.

In legal matters, since your application of the conservation approach should eliminate the need to maintain counsel on a retainer fee, call your local attorney referral service if the need for a lawyer arises. Most lawyers registered with such services offer an hour of free consultation, which should be adequate to decide whether you indeed need a lawyer or not, and if you do whether you should seek the services of a specialist in one of the branches of the legal profession (criminal, traffic, torts, taxes, etc.).

If your legal difficulty is not a complex one, you may want to settle for a recent law-school graduate, whose lack of experience is quite often compensated for by eagerness and dedication. All you normally have to do to obtain the names and phone numbers of these young legal spitfires is call a law school in your vicinity and ask if you could be referred to one of their bright young graduates. In most cases the school will be glad to oblige.

Another source of sharp attorneys at modest fees is your local federal, state, county, or city office, courthouse, and the district attorney's office. A great number of lawyers begin their careers there, the turnover is usually high, and the referral, when obtained, is certainly dependable.

Backtracking to a Point

Although it is highly inadvisable for you to attempt to perform open-heart surgery upon yourself, situations do arise where professional help is simply not to be found and you have to do the best you can without it.

Imagine yourself in the unlikely situation of being attacked by a stranger while you are vacationing in the wilderness. A scuffle follows, a shot is fired, and you find yourself standing over your assailant with *his* gun smoking in your hand. Fortunately, the man is alive, though wounded. As you kneel down next to him, he manages to deliver a kick to your jaw. The instant before you hear the crunch of a broken tooth in your mouth, you make out the sign on the man's shirt which suggests to you that he is an escapee from a mental institution. In spite of the pained jaw, you manage to keep your assailant down and tie him up.

Now, with the closest dwelling being, say, thirty miles away, you could find yourself doing a number of unwise things. Being a civilized human being, however, you find yourself backtracking in a direction you've never been before. You find yourself, being alone, acting in the capacity of your own attorney: "I have shot a man, in self-defense; he is still alive, so I must help him." Suddenly you are slipping into the role of a physician: You cater to the man's wound. A dentist: You place a wad of cotton from your first-aid kit on the jagged remnant of tooth in your mouth to keep the edges from cutting your tongue. You catch the pathetic look of madness in your assailant's eyes and you find yourself trying to reason with him: You are taking on the role of a psychiatrist.

In a matter of a few minutes you've backtracked to total self-sufficiency, you've gained control of the situation, and, in spite of the extremely tense circumstances, have managed to remain the human being that you are.

Chapter 14

End Your Money Woes

As many ways as there are for spending money, there are as many ways for spending less. And spending less, as a rule, involves nothing other than breaking innumerable habits.

Take the credit-card habit. It's one of the worst habits you can get into. It leaves you constantly open to the irresistible temptation to buy something you cannot afford to pay cash for, with interest payments raising the total price. A new washing machine, for example, that would cost you $200 if you paid cash, costs you $250 if you buy it on time—and in the end it's still cash (even if it's in the form of checks) that you part with. The credit-card habit is one of the easiest habits to get into and one of the hardest habits to break. It makes you accustomed to spending more money than you don't have over a longer period of time than you would if you had it. If it sounds illogical, it is.

One way to break the credit-card habit is to destroy all but two credit cards. Use these remaining cards *only* for identification purposes to cash checks. You will discover that there are considerably fewer items that you find essential than you did while you were using charge accounts and credit cards. Use the lay-away system to purchase larger, costlier—and absolutely essential—items. Although most stores prefer not to hold such purchases for more than 90 days, they *will* allow you up to twice that time to pay off. Make sure, however, that your intention to take more time is known to them. With the lay-away system your payment method is very similar to a charge account, only it costs nowhere near as much since there is usually no interest charge. Adopt the philosophy that if you can't afford to pay cash for something—or lay it away—you don't need it.

Make out a budget and abide by it. There are a number of family and individual budget books that may be bought for under two dollars in most stationery stores, drugstores, and supermarkets to assist you in recording your expenses on a day-to-day basis. This type of record-keeping, in addition to helping you stay solvent, comes in handy every year when income tax time rolls around.

Get into the habit of saving a portion of your check each time you get paid. Make it a standard deduction as far as you are concerned. If your take-home pay is $150 each week, see if you can manage on 90% of that. Deposit the $15 difference in your savings account. You will get used to your self-imposed cut in salary, and when vacation-time comes around you will have $780 more to enjoy it with. Of course, if you have any other reason for putting your money away—your children's education, car purchase, home improvement, retirement fund—the end result will be the same: You will have it.

Another method of spending less, if you are a cigarette smoker, is to stop smoking. It is a habit that does good neither to your financial situation nor your health. There are clinics that have been established to help you break the habit as well as a number of books that offer you ways to get out of the smokers' rut. As an incentive, drop a couple of quarters every day for each pack of cigarettes that you managed not to buy into a piggy bank. Get a large one. Place a date that is exactly a year away from the day you quit smoking on the piggy bank. When that year passes, break the bank.

You may be surprised to discover that you have anywhere between $180 and $720 worth of quarters spilling out all over your table or floor—money that you would have burned had you not stopped smoking. The amount will, of course, depend on whether you've been smoking—or, more precisely, *nonsmoking*—one, two, three, or four packs of cigarettes each day. If you've been smoking regularly for years, let the price of cigarettes and the number of packs you smoked each day determine the amount of money you slip daily into your bank at home.

You can make that money work for you, by taking it at the beginning or end of each month to a bank that pays interest and deposit it in a savings account. You may find yourself being able to retire ten years earlier than you've been figuring on because of this move.

If you find yourself habitually stopping at a newsstand and buying weekly or monthly magazines at newsstand prices, break the habit! Subscribe instead. Why pay $26 for 52 issues of *Time* magazine, for example, when *Time* magazine offers you those same 52 issues for $16.

Get in the habit of spending less money without buying less. You can do this by taking advantage of the various sales, to begin with, and by shopping in large discount stores instead of the exclusive, plush-carpeted, chandeliered outlets where the cost of the decor is passed on to you on the pricetags of the goods sold.

Make use of the coupons that constantly appear in various magazines—such as *Woman's Day*, *Family Circle*, and *Lady's Circle*—newspapers, flyers, and brochures. These offer you substantial savings on everything from a bar of soap to a complete home entertainment center.

Finally, do not be a compulsive, or impulsive, buyer. Simply because an item is on sale is not necessarily reason enough to buy it; the least you should do is find out what it is. My wife came home one day clutching an odd-looking object to her bosom. "Look what I got!" she announced enthusiastically. I looked at it, puzzled. "Don't you like it?" she asked, a note of apprehension in her voice. "Maybe I should have bought a blue one?"

"No," I said, "the color is good." I looked it over. It did have an appealing green color. "What is it?" I asked.

"I don't know," she said, "but it was on sale."

Conclusion

Shortages of one sort or another are as inevitable as changes in the weather and are usually a lot less predictable. Their causes are as diverse as they are common. Droughts, frost, floods, tornadoes destroy crops; diseases put a dent in the cattle industry, which results in meat and/or dairy product shortages; political blunders bring about a scarcity of fuel and/or minerals; economic malfunction results in inflation, recession, depression, and/or a money shortage. Most of these causes are beyond the control of the individual consumer, who is left with no choice but to find, or create, his own solutions—on the individual level.

At the same time, it pays to try to influence the government-industry monolith to act. Doing so alone is ineffective; one needs the cooperation of other consumers. Joining existing groups or forming new ones, which through the signing of petitions and other public action advises our representatives that the consumer is aware and expects action, is probably the most effective way to obtain results.

On the individual level, you the consumer need an immediate solution to each and every immediate shortage problem. You do have a shortage-solving tool in your possession—the abstract, yet practical, tool that is the Trident Principle. It is the key to survival in the Age of Shortages which, considering the current state of economic affairs and the constantly growing population problem, we are heading into at breakneck speed.

This book will have served its purpose if it has impressed upon you the potential of the Trident Principle in battling shortages of all kinds. There is no other solution to shortages: If you do not *conserve,* you waste, and if you do not produce while using, you do not have; if you do not have, you *substitute;* if there are no substitutes, you *backtrack.* It's as simple as that.

Appendix A

Room Air Conditioner Sizing Chart

Note: Estimates are for average conditions: 8 ft. ceilings, standard insulation and glass area, average people load. If kitchen is included in area, add 2,000 B.T.U.'s to your estimate. Measurements are in sq. ft.

Air Conditioner B.T.U. Rating	Average Maximum Temperature Range (°F.)		
	75—80	80—85	85—90
4,000	260—275	185—200	155—175
5,000	325—340	235—250	195—215
6,000	395—405	280—300	235—245
7,000	465—475	330—350	275—285
8,000	535—545	380—400	315—325
9,000	595—605	430—450	335—365
10,000	665—675	480—500	395—405
11,000	725—740	530—550	435—445
12,000	860—875	580—600	515—525
14,000	925—940	680—700	555—565
16,000	1065—1080	780—800	635—645
17,000	1125—1140	830—850	675—685
23,000	1525—1540	1130—1150	915—925
24,000	1595—1610	1180—1200	955—965

Air Conditioner B.T.U. Rating	Average Maximum Temperature Range (°F.)		
	90—95	95—100	100—105
4,000	140—155	125—135	90—100
5,000	180—195	160—170	115—125
6,000	215—230	195—205	135—150
7,000	255—270	230—240	160—175
8,000	295—310	265—275	185—200
9,000	325—340	295—305	205—220
10,000	365—380	330—340	230—245
11,000	400—415	360—375	255—270
12,000	475—490	425—440	305—315
14,000	510—525	460—475	325—340
16,000	590—605	530—545	375—390
17,000	625—635	560—575	400—410
23,000	850—865	760—775	540—555
24,000	890—905	795—810	565—580

Appendix B

Average Annual Electrical Energy Consumption

Appliance	Kwh	Cost
Electric toothbrush	5	$ .12
Curling iron	7	.18
Makeup mirror	7	.18
Food mixer	10	.24
Hair dryer	15	.35
Clock	17	.40
Radio (transistor)	20	.47
Hair dryer (800 watt)	23	.61
Radio/phonograph (transistor)	40	.94
Toaster	40	.94
Vacuum cleaner	45	1.06
Coffee percolator	100	2.36
Iron (hand)	150	3.54
Frying pan	240	5.66
Fluorescent light	260	6.14
Dishwasher	350	8.26
Television set (b&w)	400	9.44
Television set (color)	540	12.74
Range	1550	36.58
Light bulbs	1870	44.13
Air conditioner	2000	47.20

Appendix C

Energy Value and Nutrient Content of
Some Common Foods
(Values per 100 g)

Food Item	Energy (kcal)*	Water (g)	Protein (g)	Fat (g)	Carbo-hydrate (g)
Apple	47	84.1	0.3	trace	12.2
Beef steak (fried)	273	56.9	20.4	20.4	0
Beer (½ cup)	31	96.7	0.2	trace	2.2
Butter	793	13.9	0.4	85.1	trace
Cabbage (boiled)	9	95.7	1.3	trace	1.1
Cheese (Cheddar)	425	37.0	25.4	34.5	trace
Haddock (fried)	175	65.1	20.4	8.3	3.6
Milk (fresh, whole)	66	87.0	3.4	3.7	4.8
Orange (with peel)	27	64.8	0.6	trace	6.4
Peas (canned)	86	72.7	5.9	trace	16.5
Potatoes (raw)	70	80.0	2.5	trace	15.9
Rice (raw)	361	11.7	6.2	1.0	86.8
Spirits (whiskey 70 proof, gin)*	222	63.5	trace	0	trace
White bread	243	38.3	7.8	1.4	52.7
Whole wheat bread	339	15.0	13.6	2.5	69.1

*Kinetic calories

Appendix D

Recommended Daily Intake of Energy and Nutrients

Age Range	Weight (lbs.)	Energy (kcal)	Protein (gms)	Iron (mg)	Calcium (mg)
Infants					
0-2 mos	9	54.5/lb	1.0/lb	6	0.4
2-6	15	50.0/lb	0.9/lb	10	0.5
6 mos-1 yr	20	45.5/lb	0.8/lb	15	0.6
Children					
1-2 yrs	26	1,100	25	15	0.7
2-3	31	1,250	25	15	0.8
3-4	35	1,400	30	10	0.8
4-6	42	1,600	30	10	0.8
6-8	51	2,000	35	10	0.9
8-10	62	2,200	40	10	1.0
Boys					
10-12 yrs	77	2,500	45	10	1.2
12-14	95	2,700	50	18	1.4
14-18	130	3,000	60	18	1.4
Girls					
10-12	77	2,250	50	18	1.2
12-14	97	2,300	50	18	1.3
14-18	117	2,400	55	18	1.3
Men					
18-22	147	2,800	60	10	0.8
22-35	154	2,800	65	10	0.8
35-55	154	2,600	65	10	0.8
55-75+	154	2,400	65	10	0.8
Women					
18-22	128	2,000	55	18	0.8
22-35	128	2,000	55	18	0.8
35-55	128	1,850	55	18	0.8
55-75+	128	1,700	55	10	0.8
pregnant	......+	200	+10	18	+0.4
lactating	......+	1,000	+20	18	+0.5

Appendix E

Remommended Daily Intake of Vitamins

Age Range	Weight (lbs.)	A (I.U.)	B-1 (thiamine) (mg)	B-2 (riboflavin) (mg)	Niacin (mg)	C (ascorbic acid) (mg)
Infants
0-2 mos	9	1,500	0.2	0.4	5	35
2-6	15	1,500	0.4	0.5	7	35
6 mos-1 yr	20	1,500	0.5	0.6	8	35
Children
1-2 yrs	26	2,000	0.6	0.6	8	40
2-3	31	2,000	0.6	0.7	8	40
3-4	35	2,500	0.7	0.8	9	40
4-6	42	2,500	0.8	0.9	11	40
6-8	51	3,500	1.0	1.1	13	40
8-10	62	3,500	1.1	1.2	15	40
Boys
10-12	77	4,500	1.3	1.3	17	40
12-14	95	5,000	1.4	1.4	18	45
14-18	130	5,000	1.5	1.5	20	55
Girls
10-12	77	4,500	1.1	1.3	15	40
12-14	97	5,000	1.2	1.4	15	45
14-18	117	5,000	1.2	1.5	16	50
Men
18-22	147	5,000	1.4	1.6	18	60
22-35	154	5,000	1.4	1.7	18	60
35-55	154	5,000	1.3	1.7	17	60
55-75+	154	5,000	1.2	1.7	14	60
Women
18-22	128	5,000	1.0	1.5	13	55
22-35	128	5,000	1.0	1.5	13	55
35-55	128	5,000	1.0	1.5	13	55
55-75+	128	5,000	1.0	1.5	13	55
pregnant	......	+1,000	+0.1	+0.3	+ 2	+ 5
lactating	......	+2,000	+0.5	+0.5	+ 7	+ 5

Index

A

Air conditioning,
  energy consumption in
    1973, 31
  proper rating of, 31-33
  location of units, 36
  types of, 29, 30
Air leakage,
  check for, 24, 25
Antares Engineering, 68
Apartment dwellers,
  and energy conserva-
    tion, 38-40
"Artificial rain" system,
  house cooling with, 38

Attic,
  insulation of, 35, 36
Automobiles,
  electric and foot-
    powered, 66-68
  function of, 56, 57
  introduction of, 55
  purchasing of, 56-61

B

Backtracking,
  re air conditioning, 30
  re fishing, 89, 90
  re home furnishings,
    146

166

re hunting, 89, 90
re locomotion, 68, 69
re professional serv-
ices, 152, 153
re refrigerators, 49
re shortages, 80
as solution to short-
ages, 82
Beaumont, Robert G., 67
Boating, 136
Breakfast,
varieties of, 90-93
Beef cuts,
grouping of, 78
"British thermal units,"
(B.T.U.),
capacity for cooling,
32, 33
definition of, 31

C

Callenbach, Ernest, 132
Canadian Sailing, 136
Canned goods,
alternatives in, 79
Car and Driver, 59
Car Pooling,
re conservation, 64
Cars,
electric and foot-
powered, 66-68
Cars, Economy,
gas mileage of, 60, 61
price of, 60, 61
seating capacity of, 60
selection of, 59-61

Carrier, Dr. Willis H., 29
Cereal mix,
preparation of, 92
Changing Times, 117
CityCar, The, 67
Citizen's Advisory
Committee in Environ-
mental Quality,
re energy consumption
in 1973, 31, 52
Communal Living,
concept of, 133-135
example of kibbutzim,
134
example of Tasaday
tribe, 135, 136
Conservation,
re air conditioning, 30
by apartment dwellers,
38, 40
re cooking, 85, 95
re driving, 64-69
re fuel, 45, 62
re food shortage, 74-77
re heating, 21, 23
re home furnishings,
142-144
re lighting, 40, 41
re locomotion, 68
re professional serv-
ices, 149, 150
as solution to short-
ages, 20
re water, 99-104
Consumers Union of the
U.S., 59, 60

Cooking,
  process of, 89-95
  timing of, 45-47
Cugnot, Nicholas Joseph,
  55

D

Dairy products,
  re substitution, 49
Department of Motor
  Vehicles,
  minimum power re-
    quirement set by, 65
Dinner,
  varieties in, 93, 94
Drapes,
  energy conservation
    by, 25
Driving,
  alternatives to, 64-69

E

Eggs,
  preparation of, 90, 91
Electrical appliances,
  small,
  energy consumption by,
    49, 50
Electrical Industries
  Association of
  Southern California, 33
Electricity,
  cars powered by, 66-69
Energy crisis,
  in the kitchen, 51
  solutions to, 20, 33

Entertainment,
  sources of, 51-54
Environmental Protection
  Agency, 27, 59

F

Family Circle, 68, 87
Fireplace,
  function of, 26, 27
Fishing,
  re backtracking, 89, 90
Food shortage,
  alternatives during,
    74-80
  varieties of, 74
Flowerpots,
  planting in, 87, 88
Fresh produce,
  alternatives in, 79
  growing of, 82-88
Frozen foods,
  alternatives in, 79
Fuel,
  conservation of, 45
Furnace,
  size and rating of,
    21, 22

G

Gardening,
  varieties of, 81-88
Gasoline,
  conservation of, 62-64
Geothermal Research
  and Development,
  appropriations for,
    28, 29

Go Boating, 136

H

Harvey, Jenifer, 61
Heating outlets,
  control of, 26
Herbert, George, 74
Home Furnishings,
  conserving of, 142-144
  construction of, 145-146
  selection of, 141
  substitutions of, 144
Home ownership,
  factors involved in,
    117, 121
*Homeowner's Survival
  Kit, The*, 23
House trailers,
  cost of, 133
  property for, 132
  selection of, 130, 131
Houseboats,
  building of, 136
  plans for, 136
  selection of, 135-138
Household items,
  alternatives in, 79, 80
Houses, building of,
  actual work involved,
    128, 129
  construction of, 127
  cost of, 128
  design of, 125, 126
  factors involved in,
    122-124
  financing of, 125

  location for, 126
Houses, Purchased,
  alternatives to, 121
  expenditures for,
    210-221
  location of, 121
  mortgage of, 120
  price increase of,
    116, 117
  selection of, 118-120
Houses, Rental,
  alternatives in, 115
  availability of, 107-109
  finding of, 110, 111
  function of, 112
  percentage of income
    spent on, 115
  re *rental duration*, 113
  suitability of, 114, 115
Hunting,
  re backtracking, 89, 90

I

Insulation,
  re air conditioning, 34
  function of, 23, 24
  re heating, 23, 24

J

Jenatzy, Camille, 66

K

*Kiplinger's Family Buy-
  ing Guide*, 117, 118

L

Lakeland Boating, 136
Light bulbs,
  replacement of wattage,
    41, 42
Lighting,
  backtracking for, 44
  conservation of, 40, 41
  substitution for, 41, 43
Living Poor With Style,
  132
Lunch,
  varieties of, 93
Los Angeles Times, 124

M

Meals,
  planning of, 47, 74, 89,
    90
Meat,
  preparation of, 90, 91
Mercedes-Benz,
  re LE 306 Electro-
    Transporter, 67
Mirror surfaces,
  to conserve electricity,
    41, 43
Mobile homes,
  cost of, 132, 133
  depreciation of, 131
  property for, 132
  selection of, 130, 131
Money woes, solutions to,
  re breaking of habits,
    ie, compulsive buy-
      ing, 157

    ie, credit cards, 154,
      155
    ie, smoking, 156
  re budgeting, 155
  re coupon savings, 157
  re discount savings,
    157
  re lay-away purchas-
    ing, 155
  re magazine subscrip-
    tions, 156, 157
  re sales savings, 157
  re savings accounts,
    155, 156
*Motor Boating and
  Sailing*, 136
Motor Trend, 59
Motorcycling,
  re conservation, 65, 66

N

National Science Founda-
  tion, 27
Nutrition,
  awareness of, 74

P

Pancakes,
  preparation of, 92
People Powered Vehicle,
  68
Planting,
  areas for, 86
  instructions for, 87, 88
  times for vegetables,
    82-86

Property, Residential,
   location of, 121
   price increase of, 117
   selection of, 118, 120
Population,
   increase in, 73, 97, 98
Professional Services,
   backtracking for, 152,
      153
   conservation in, 149,
      150
   obtainment of, 148-150
   substitution for,
      150-152
Public Transit,
   re conservation in, 64,
      65

R

Refrigerator-freezer,
   care of, 49
   use of, 47, 48
Residence, Standard,
   alternatives to, 130-138
Road Test, 59
Room Air Conditioner
   Sizing Chart, 33
Rudder, 136

S

Saab,
   re electrical delivery
      van, 67
Sail, 136
Seafood Rice Salad,
   preparation of, 94

Seawater-desalting
   plants,
   operation of, 98, 99
Sebring-Vanguard, 67
Shade,
   house cooling by, 37
Skelsey, Alice, 87
Soap,
   use of, 80
Solar energy,
   harnessing of, 27, 28
Soup,
   preparation of, 92
Storm windows,
   types of, 25
Substitution,
   re cooling systems, 37,
      38
   re food shortage, 77-80
   re home furnishings,
      145, 146
   re lighting, 42, 43
   re locomotion, 68
   re professional serv-
      ices, 150, 151
   re refrigerators, 49
   as solution to short-
      ages, 20
   re standard residence,
      130-138
   re television, 52-54
Supermarkets,
   shortages at, 72-74

T

Television,

energy consumed by, 52
substitution for, 52-54
Thermostat setting,
  in air conditioning, 34
  in heating, 34
  proper selection of, 22,
    23
Time magazine, 49, 50,
  117-120
"Trash heaps,"
  as source of power, 27
Trident Principle,
  re air conditioning, 29,
    30, 37
  re cooking, 45, 89
  definition of, 20
  re entertainment, 51,
    52
  re food shortage, 73
  re heating, 21, 26, 29
  re home furnishings,
    142
  re housing, 109
  re lighting, 40, 43
  re locomotion, 68
  re meal planning, 89
  re professional serv-
    ices, 148
  re water, 98
TV Guide, 52

U

United States Geological
  Survey,
  on water, 96, 97
U.S. News & World
Report, 27

V

Vegetables,
  growing of, 81-88
  planting times for,
    beets, 84
    broccoli, 83
    bush beans, 86
    cabbage, 84
    carrots, 85
    cucumbers, 86
    lettuce, 84, 85
    onions, 85
    parsley, 85
    peas, 84
    spinach, 82, 83
    swiss chard, 85
    tomatoes, 85
    zucchini, 86

W

Waffles,
  preparation of, 92
Water,
  in agriculture, 98
  conservation of,
    in bathing, 100-102
    in food preparation,
      99, 100
    in fountains, 104
    in gardening, 102,
      103
    in sanitation, 102
    in swimming pools,
      103

consumption of, 97, 98
in domestic use, 99
estimated supply of,
  96, 97
in industry, 99
"returnable percent-
  age" of, 98
Water-reclamation
  projects,
  actualization of, 99
Water-sprinkler system,
  house cooling by, 38
Watkins, A. M., 22, 23
Weather stripping,
  installment of, 24, 25
Window boxes,
  planting in, 87, 88